英語総合力・完全トレーニング

Reading

Listening

4

Writing

Speaking

in

4 skills in one book

ONE

フォー・イン・ワン

advanced 上級

霜村和久 著

アルク

はじめに

聞きっぱなし、読みっぱなしにしない

　英語学習では「読む」「聞く」「書く」「話す」の四技能が必要——これは古くからよく言われていることですが、実際にはインプットしたものを理解しないと始まらないという考えから、多くの場合、「読む」と「聞く」に重点が置かれます。特に、難解な英文を理解できたり、スピードの速い英文を聞き取れたりすると、「ああ、勉強したな」という満足感を得られたりします。そして、そこで止まってしまう。英語を教えていると、習熟度や学習期間に関係なく、そうした傾向がさまざまな場面で見受けられます。

　しかし、「四技能」とはあくまでも便宜上の区分け。日本語のことを考えてもおわかりのように、別々に存在しているわけではありません。読んだり聞いたりしたものを、さらに書いたり話したりしてはじめて、言葉を運用していると言えるのです。

　長年英語に触れてきたみなさんの頭の中には、膨大な量の英語データが存在しているはずです。しかし、実際にアウトプットして運用しているのはその数分の1、ひょっとしたら数十分の1かもしれません。

　そうした技能の不均衡状態を解消するのが、4つの技能を一冊で学べるこの 4-in-ONE シリーズです。本書では、「学校英語の枠を超えた自然な英語」を題材に、「自分で使うこと」を最終目的にした学習が展開されます。語彙力、表現力だけではなく、英語の運用力を伸ばす。その意識を持って最後のページまで進んでいってください。

　英語はみなさんにとって a foreign language（外国の言語）ではなく、a second language（第二の言語）です。本書を通じて、実践に役立つ第二言語としての英語を身につけていただければ幸いです。

2021年3月　　霜村和久

Contents

Listening を鍛える!

Chapter 1　聞いた情報を相手に伝える　基礎編

Chapter 2　聞いた情報を相手に伝える　上級編

Reading を鍛える！

Chapter 3　読んだ情報を相手に伝える　基礎編

この本の使い方

この本は、大きく、前半の「Listeningを鍛える!」と後半の「Readingを鍛える!」に分かれ、それぞれ10のUnitから成ります。学習を始める前に、1つのUnitの構成と学習手順について、しっかり確認しましょう。

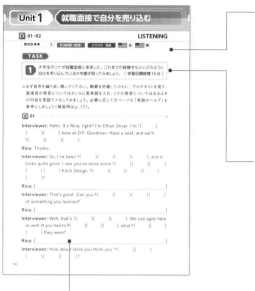

①学習する英語の種類を知る：このUnitで聞く、あるいは読む英語の「難易度」「長さ」「素材の形式」「ナレーターの国籍と性別」を示します（「ナレーターの国籍と性別」表記はListeningのUnitのみです）。またヘッドホン 🎧 のマークがついている箇所は、音声を聞きます。

②聞く・読む英語と「TASK」を知る：これから聞く、あるいは読む英語はどういう状況で発信されていて、あなたはどういう目的を持ってインプットすべきか、また、インプットした後に何をすべきかが説明されています。学習目標時間を目安に学習してみましょう（あくまでも目安ですので、必ずしもこの時間内に終わらせる必要はありません）。

③「TASK」に取り組む：音声を聞き（あるいは読み）、与えられた課題（TASK）に取り組みましょう。一度聞いたり読んだりした後にTASKが完了できない場合には、「単語のヘルプ」を参照して、もう一度、チャレンジしてみましょう（なお、Listeningは冒頭にTASKがありますが、Readingは、「単語のヘルプ」の後にTASKがあります。

● TASK の役割 ●

従来の英語学習では、「リスニング／リーディング力がある」とは、「一度で正確に聞ける」「速く、正確に読める」ことを、「スピーキング／ライティング力がある」とは「その場で正しく、適切な話し方ができる」「正確に伝わる書き方ができる」ことをそれぞれ指していたかもしれません。

　しかし、現実のコミュニケーションでは、「読んで理解して終わり」「言いたいことを伝えて終わり」のように一つの技能だけで完結するケースは多くありません。例えば、誰かの言ったことを聞いて、それに応答する、何かを読んで、要点をメモに取る、といったように、「聞く」＋「話す」、「読む」＋「書く」という技能の統合が頻繁に起こります。

　この4-in-ONEシリーズでは、「聞いた」あとに話す／書くTASK、「読んだ」あとに話す／書くTASKを与えてトレーニングを積み重ねます。TASKに取り組むことで、複数の技能を組み合わせながら、コミュニケーションのツールとしての英語の運用力、自己表現力を伸ばしましょう。

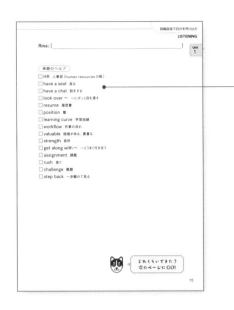

④「単語のヘルプ」を使う：この Unit の英文の中で、難易度が特に高いもの、あるいは固有名詞、気を付けるべきイディオムなどを取り上げています。インプットの補助に使いましょう（Reading では、他にわからないものがあった場合には、書き抜いて、辞書で調べておきましょう）。

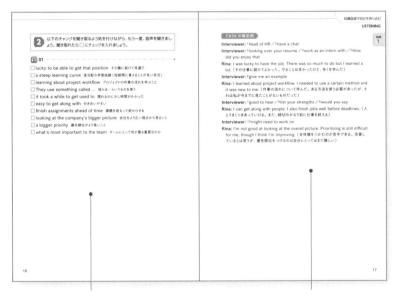

⑤チャンクを追いながら聞く（Listening のみ）：「TASK」が完了できなかった場合は、チャンク（意味を成す、複数の単語のかたまり）を目で追いながら、音声を聞きましょう。聞き取れたものにはチェックを入れます。「TASK」をすでに完了した方も、内容の確認のために、チャンクを意識して改めて聞きましょう。

⑥「TASK の解答（例）」で答え合わせ：「解答例」とある場合には、一つの例として参照してください。音声マークがあるものは、よく聞き、指示のあるものは口に出して練習しましょう。

3 聞き取りの解説

ここでは、面接でよく使われる表現にすぐ対応することと、うまく自分を売りこむことがポイントです。

※ 質問を聞きすぎない

How did you enjoy that?

リナが履歴書に書いたインターン体験について、感想を聞いている表現です。

一般的には、

How was it?

と聞くところですが、ここでは「それをどのように楽しみましたか」と尋ねています。なお、enjoy という単語が使われてはいても、楽しかったことだけを選んで答える必要はありません。リナのように、苦労した話を含めてもけっこうです。

If you had to list your strengths, what would you say they were?

「もしあなたがご自分の長所を一覧にしなければならないとなれば、それがどんなものだとおっしゃいますか」と言っていますが、結局は、何が自分の長所と思っているかを尋ねている質問です。

いつもいつも簡単に、

What are your strengths?

と言ってくれるわけではありませんので、注意が必要です。ただ、list ... strengths ... what ... they were さえ聞き取れば、意味の推測は十分可能です。

※ つなぎ言葉に注目する

質問を聞いてすぐに「きれいな」答えを返せるとは限りません。しかし、返答に詰まって黙ってしまうのは最も避けたいこと。そこで、

How did you enjoy that?

に対しては、まず、

Oh, that was great.

と言い、また、

Can you give me an example ...?

に対しては、

There's so much.

と言ってから、さらに、

Let me think

と続け、その間に頭の中で答えをまとめています。

※ 控えめな表現にも注目する

「英語では直接的な物言いをする」と言われますが、それは自分の主張を前面に出し過ぎることは言わないのです。

I'd like to think I'm easy to get along with ...

がその一例。長所を聞かれていますが、いきなり自分が売りこみたい性格だけを答えるのではなく、I'd like to think (that)...（…と思いたいのです）をクッションとして使うことで、柔らかい感じを出しています。

Tips すぐに応用したい表現

for one thing（一つには）
→これに対して、for another thing（また別に）と続くこともあります。
I mean（つまり）
→「そうではなく」の意味もあります。
... as well（... も）
→文末につけます。
rather than ...（... ではなく）
→対比させる形（ここでは finish に対する leave）が続きます。
can sometimes be ...（時には ... ということもある）
→ is や are では断定し過ぎると思われるときに使います。
I'm getting better at it.（うまくなってきています）
→ be good at の be が get に、good が比較級の better になった形です。

4 では英文を見ながら、もう一度、聞きましょう。

🔊 01

Interviewer: Hello. It's Rina, right? I'm Ethan Oliver. I'm head of HR here at D.F. Goodman. Have a seat, and we'll have a chat.

Rina: Thanks.

Interviewer: So, I've been looking over your resume, and it looks quite good. I see you've done some work as an intern with Kitch Design. How did you enjoy that?

Rina: Oh, that was great. I felt so lucky to be able to get that position while I was still finishing my degree. There was a steep learning curve, but I learned a lot there.

Interviewer: That's great. Can you give me an example of something you learned?

Rina: Oh, wow, OK. There's so much. Let me think For one thing just learning about project workflow was valuable. I mean, new projects there aren't structured like I imagined a traditional office would be. They use something called "agile flow" for project development. I'd never heard of it before, and it took a while to get used to.

Interviewer: Well, that's good to hear. We use agile here as well. If you had to list your strengths, what would you say they were?

Rina: I'd like to think I'm easy to get along with, so that's one thing Hmm ... and I prefer to finish assignments ahead of time rather than leave them until I have to rush things.

Interviewer: How about skills you think you might need to work on?

Rina: Hmm ... I guess looking at the company's bigger picture can sometimes be a challenge. Once or twice, I was really focused on a job that was challenging me, only to be told I didn't need to worry

---

⑦「聞き方、読み方」のコツを読む：「TASK」を遂行するためのポイント、また、英文全体を聞いたり読んだりして、理解するための語句や文法を解説しています。

⑧ Tips を活用する：表現の幅を広げたり、会話を膨らませたりするための例文を取り上げています。コミュニケーションに活用しましょう。

⑨ スクリプトを見ながら聞く（Listening のみ）：英文スクリプトと日本語訳を見ながら、理解できているか確認しましょう。

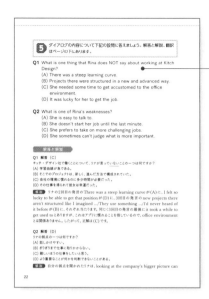

⑩四択問題：聞いたり読んだりした内容について、2つの四択問題にトライ。できなかった場合には、もう一度、英文に戻りましょう。

⑪ポーズ入り音声：スラッシュの単位で区切って復習します。ポーズの箇所で口に出してみましょう。

※英文に出てくる固有名詞や統計データを含むいかなる情報も、現実のものとは関係ありません。

音声ダウンロードの方法

本書では、音声マーク（ 01 ）の付いた箇所の英文や会話文の音声が聞けます。以下の方法で、無料でダウンロードできます。本書の学習にお役立てください。

パソコンをご利用の場合

「アルク・ダウンロードセンター」 https://www.alc.co.jp/dl/ から音声がダウンロードできます。書籍名（『4-in-ONE advanced 上級』）、または商品コード（7021029）で本書の音声を検索し、画面の指示に従って操作してください。

スマートフォンをご利用の場合

学習用無料アプリ「booco」 https://www.booco.jp/ をご利用ください。「booco」のインストール方法は表紙カバー袖でご案内しています。インストール後、ホーム画面下「探す」から、書籍名（『4-in-ONE advanced 上級』）、または商品コード（7021029）で本書を検索し、音声ファイルをダウンロードしてください。

本サービスの内容は、予告なく変更する場合がございます。あらかじめご了承ください。

Listening を鍛える!

Chapter 1
聞いた情報を相手に伝える　基礎編

ここでは、以下のようなダイアログ（2～3名のやりとり）を素材に学習します。発言者ひとりひとりの主張をしっかりつかみながら、一度で理解できない場合は、繰り返し聞いてみましょう。

Unit 1　就職面接で自分を売り込む
〈ビジネス／面接〉

Unit 2　働き方は十人十色
〈ビジネス／日常会話（3人）〉

Unit 3　仕事と家事と子育てと
〈日常／夫婦の会話〉

Unit 4　技を極める
〈技術／インタビュー〉

Unit 5　生活にもっと緑を
〈新規ビジネス／インタビュー〉

🎧 01-02   **LISTENING**

| 難易度 ●●○○○ 2 | | 約300語（普通） | | ビジネス／面接 | | 🇺🇸 女 | | 🇺🇸 男 |

TASK

1 大学生のリナが就職面接に来ました。これまでの経験をもとにどのように
自分を売り込んでいるかを聞き取ってみましょう。 [**学習目標時間15分**]

●まず音声を繰り返し聞いてください。概要を把握したのちに、下のテキストを見て、
面接官の発言についてはカッコに英単語を入れ、リナの発言についてはおおよそ
の内容を英語でメモしてみましょう。必要に応じて次ページの「単語のヘルプ」も
参考にしましょう（解答例はp. 17）。

🎧 01 ─────────────────────────────◆

Interviewer: Hello. It's Rina, right? I'm Ethan Oliver. I'm 1(   )
(   )(   ) here at D.F. Goodman. Have a seat, and we'll
2(   )(   )(   ).

Rina: Thanks.

Interviewer: So, I've been 3(   )(   )(   )(   ), and it
looks quite good. I see you've done some 4(   )(   )(   )
(   ) (   ) Kitch Design. 5(   )(   )(   )(   )
(   )?

Rina: [_____]

Interviewer: That's great. Can you 6(   )(   )(   )(   )
of something you learned?

Rina: [_____]

Interviewer: Well, that's 7(   )(   )(   ). We use agile here
as well. If you had to 8(   )(   )(   ), what 9(   )(   )
(   ) they were?

Rina: [_____]

Interviewer: How about skills you think you 10(   )(   )
(   )(   )(   )?

Rina: [_____]

(単語のヘルプ)

☐ HR　人事部（human resources の略）

☐ have a seat　座る

☐ have a chat　話をする

☐ look over 〜　〜にざっと目を通す

☐ resume　履歴書

☐ position　職

☐ learning curve　学習曲線

☐ workflow　作業の流れ

☐ valuable　価値がある、貴重な

☐ strength　長所

☐ get along with 〜　〜とうまく付き合う

☐ assignment　課題

☐ rush　急ぐ

☐ challenge　難題

☐ step back　一歩離れて見る

どれくらいできた？
次のページに GO!

2 以下のチャンクを聞き取るよう気を付けながら、もう一度、音声を聞きましょう。聞き取れたら □ にチェックを入れましょう。

🎧 **01** ···◆

☐ lucky to be able to get that position　その職に就けて幸運だ

☐ a steep learning curve　急勾配の学習曲線（短期間に覚えることが多い状況）

☐ learning about project workflow　プロジェクトの作業の流れを学ぶこと

☐ They use something called ...　彼らは…というものを使う

☐ it took a while to get used to　慣れるのに少し時間がかかった

☐ easy to get along with　付き合いやすい

☐ finish assignments ahead of time　課題を前もって終わらせる

☐ looking at the company's bigger picture　会社をより広い視点から見ること

☐ a bigger priority　優先順位がより高いこと

☐ what's most important to the team　チームにとって何が最も重要なのか

TASKの解答例

Interviewer: ¹head of HR ／ ²have a chat

Interviewer: ³looking over your resume ／ ⁴work as an intern with ／ ⁵How did you enjoy that

Rina: I was lucky to have the job. There was so much to do but I learned a lot.（その仕事に就けてよかった。やることは多かったけど、多くを学んだ）

Interviewer: ⁶give me an example

Rina: I learned about project workflow. I needed to use a certain method called "agile flow" and it was new to me.（作業の流れについて学んだ。「アジャイルフロー」という方法を使う必要があったが、それは私が今までに見たことがないものだった）

Interviewer: ⁷good to hear ／ ⁸list your strengths ／ ⁹would you say

Rina: I can get along with people. I also finish jobs well before deadlines.（人とうまくつきあっていける。また、締切のかなり前に仕事を終える）

Interviewer: ¹⁰might need to work on

Rina: I'm not good at looking at the overall picture. Prioritizing is still difficult for me, though I think I'm improving.（全体像をつかむのが苦手である。改善しているとは思うが、優先順位をつけるのは自分にとってはまだ難しい）

3 聞き取りの解説

ここでは、面接でよく使われる表現にすぐ対応することと、うまく自分を売りこむことがポイントです。

● **質問を聞き逃さない**

How did you enjoy that?

リナが履歴書に書いたインターン体験について、感想を聞いている表現です。
一般的には、

How was it?

と聞くところですが、ここでは、「それをどのように楽しみましたか」と尋ねています。なお、enjoyという単語が使われてはいても、楽しかったことだけを選んで答える必要はありません。リナのように、苦労した話を含めてもけっこうです。

If you had to list your strengths, what would you say they were?

「もしあなたがご自分の長所を一覧にしなければならないとなれば、それがどんなものだとおっしゃいますか」と言っていますが、結局は、何が自分の長所と思っているかを尋ねている質問です。
いつもいつも簡単に、

What are your strengths?

と言ってくれるわけではありませんので、注意が必要です。ただ、list ... strengths ... what ... they were さえ聞き取れれば、意味の推測は十分可能です。

● **つなぎ言葉に注目する**

質問を聞いてすぐに「きれいな」答えを返せるとは限りません。しかし、返答に窮して黙ってしまうのは最も避けたいこと。そこで、

How did you enjoy that?

に対しては、まず、

Oh, that was great.

と、また、

Can you give me an example ...?

に対しては、

There's so much.

と言ってから、さらに、

Let me think.

と続け、その間に頭の中で答えをまとめています。

● 控えめな表現にも注目する

「英語では直接的な物言いをする」と言われますが、それは自分の主張を前面に出し過ぎることとは異なります。

I'd like to think I'm easy to get along with ...

がその一例。長所を聞かれていますが、いきなり自分が売り込みたい性格だけを答えるのではなく、I'd like to think (that)...（…と思いたいのです）をクッションとして使うことで、柔らかい感じを出しています。

 すぐに応用したい表現

for one thing（一つには）
→これに対して、for another thing（また別に）と続くこともあります。
I mean（つまり）
→「そうではなく」の意味もあります。
... as well（…も）
→文末につけます。
rather than ...（…ではなく）
→対比させる形（ここでは finish に対する leave）が続きます。
can sometimes be ...（時には…ということもある）
→ is や are では断定し過ぎると思われるときに使います。
I'm getting better at it.（うまくなってきています）
→ be good at の be が get に、good が比較級の better になった形です。

4 では英文を見ながら、もう一度、聞きましょう。

01

Interviewer: Hello. It's Rina, right? I'm Ethan Oliver. I'm head of HR here at D.F. Goodman. Have a seat, and we'll have a chat.

Rina: Thanks.

Interviewer: So, I've been looking over your resume, and it looks quite good. I see you've done some work as an intern with Kitch Design. How did you enjoy that?

Rina: Oh, that was great. I felt so lucky to be able to get that position while I was still finishing my degree. There was a steep learning curve, but I learned a lot there.

Interviewer: That's great. Can you give me an example of something you learned?

Rina: Oh, wow. OK. There's so much. Let me think … For one thing, just learning about project workflow was valuable. I mean, new projects there aren't structured like I imagined a traditional office would be. They use something called "agile flow" for project development. I'd never heard of it before, and it took a while to get used to.

Interviewer: Well, that's good to hear. We use agile here as well. If you had to list your strengths, what would you say they were?

Rina: I'd like to think I'm easy to get along with, so that's one thing. Hmm … and I prefer to finish assignments ahead of time rather than leave them until I have to rush things.

Interviewer: How about skills you think you might need to work on?

Rina: Hmm … I guess looking at the company's bigger picture can sometimes be a challenge. Once or twice, I was really focused on a job that was challenging me, only to be told I didn't need to worry about it so much because something else was a bigger priority overall. I need to make sure I'm stepping back now and then to see what's most important to the team. But I'm getting better at it.

日本語訳

面接官：こんにちは。リナさんですね。イーサン・オリバーです。私はここD.F.グッドマン社の人事部長です。おかけになって、お話ししましょう。

リナ：ありがとうございます。

面接官：履歴書を拝見しておりましたが、すばらしいですね。あなたはインターンとしてキッチ・デザイン社で仕事をされたということで。お仕事は楽しかったですか？

リナ：とてもよかったです。学位を取得する前にその職に就けたのはとても幸運だと思いました。仕事に習熟するのは大変でしたが、私はそこで多くのことを学びました。

面接官：それはすばらしい。例えばどんなことを学びましたか？

リナ：ああ、そうですね。ええ。たくさんあります。えーと…ひとつには、プロジェクトの作業の流れを学ぶだけでも価値がありました。つまり、その会社の新しいプロジェクトの体系は、私が想像していた従来の仕事とは異なりました。その会社ではプロジェクト開発に「アジャイルフロー」と呼ばれるものを使います。それまで聞いたこともないものでしたし、慣れるのにしばらく時間がかかりました。

面接官：あ、それはいいことを聞きました。ここでもアジャイルを使っています。もしご自分の長所を挙げるとしたら、何だと思いますか？

リナ：私は自分のことを付き合いやすい人間だと思っていたいので、それがひとつです。えー…それに、課題については、急いでやらなければならない時まで手をつけずにおくよりも、前もって終わらせたいほうです。

面接官：取り組む必要があると思うスキルについてはどうですか？

リナ：えー…会社をより広い視点から見るのは難しいと思うことがあります。一度か二度、困難な仕事にかなり集中してしたときのことですが、結局、全体的に見れば他のことのほうが優先順位が高いので、それほど気にかける必要はないことだと言わただけでした。チームにとって何が最も重要なのかを理解するために、時々、自分が一歩離れて見ているかを、確認する必要があります。でも、そうしたこともだんだん得意になってきました。

ダイアログの内容について下記の設問に答えましょう。解答と解説、翻訳はページの下にあります。

Q1 What is one thing that Rina does NOT say about working at Kitch Design?
(A) There was a steep learning curve.
(B) Projects there were structured in a new and advanced way.
(C) She needed some time to get accustomed to the office environment.
(D) It was lucky for her to get the job.

Q2 What is one of Rina's weaknesses?
(A) She is easy to talk to.
(B) She doesn't start her job until the last minute.
(C) She prefers to take on more challenging jobs.
(D) She sometimes can't judge what is more important.

解答と解説

Q1 解答（C）
キッチ・デザイン社で働くことについて、リナが言っていないことの一つは何ですか?
(A) 学習曲線が急だった。
(B) そこでのプロジェクトは、新しく、進んだ方法で構成されていた。
(C) 会社の環境に慣れるのに多少時間が必要だった。
(D) その仕事を得られて彼女は幸運だった。

解説 リナの2回目の発言のThere was a steep learning curveが(A)に、I felt so lucky to be able to get that positionが(D)に、3回目の発言のnew projects there aren't structured like I imagined .../They use something .../I'd never heard of it beforeが(B)に、それぞれ当たります。同じく3回目の発言の最後にit took a while to get used toとありますが、これは「アジャイルフロー」に慣れることを指しているので、office environmentとは関係ありません。したがって、正解は(C)です。

Q2 解答（D）
リナの弱点の一つは何ですか?
(A) 話しかけやすい。
(B) ぎりぎりまで仕事に取りかからない。
(C) 難しいほうの仕事をしたいと思う。
(D) より重要なことが何かを判断できないことがある。

解説 自分の弱点を聞かれたリナは、looking at the company's bigger picture can sometimes be a challenge（会社をより広い視点から見るのが難しい場合がある）と答えているので、これを「より重要なことが何かを判断できないことがある」と言い換えた (D) が正解です。

---

6 次に、スラッシュの箇所でリピートしてみます。意味を頭の中で映像化しつつ、流暢に言えるようになることが目標です。

🎧 02 ⋯⋯⋯⋯⋯⋯⋯⋯⋯⋯⋯⋯⋯⋯⋯⋯⋯⋯⋯⋯⋯⋯⋯⋯⋯⋯⋯⋯⋯◆

Interviewer: Hello. // It's Rina, right? // I'm Ethan Oliver. // I'm head of HR / here at D.F. Goodman. // Have a seat, / and we'll have a chat. //

Rina: Thanks. //

Interviewer: So, I've been looking over your resume, / and it looks quite good. // I see you've done some work / as an intern with Kitch Design. // How did you enjoy that? //

Rina: Oh, that was great. // I felt so lucky / to be able to get that position / while I was still finishing my degree. // There was a steep learning curve, / but I learned a lot there. //

Interviewer: That's great. // Can you give me an example / of something you learned? //

Rina: Oh, wow. // OK. // There's so much. // Let me think ... // For one thing, / just learning about project workflow was valuable. // I mean, / new projects there aren't structured / like I imagined a traditional office would be. // They use something called "agile flow" / for project development. // I'd never heard of it before, / and it took a while / to get used to. //

Interviewer: Well, that's good to hear. // We use agile here as well. // If you had to list your strengths, / what would you say they were? //

Rina: I'd like to think / I'm easy to get along with, / so that's one thing. // Hmm ... / and I prefer to finish assignments ahead of time / rather than leave them / until I have to rush things. //

Interviewer: How about skills / you think you might need to work on? //

Rina: Hmm ... / I guess looking at the company's bigger picture / can sometimes be a challenge. // Once or twice, / I was really focused on a job / that was challenging me, / only to be told / I didn't need to worry about it so much / because something else was a bigger priority overall. // I need to make sure / I'm stepping back now and then / to see what's most important to the team. // But I'm getting better at it. //

よくがんばりました！

03-04　　　　　　　　　　　　　　　**LISTENING**

| 難易度 ●●○○○ 2 | 約470語（やや長い） | ビジネス／日常会話 | 🇺🇸 女 | 🇺🇸 男2人 |

TASK

1　あなたは会社で働いています。入社してすでに年月が経ち、自分のペースで仕事を行える部分も出てきました。今後、どのように働いていきたいかを考えてみましょう。　　　　　　　　　　　[学習目標時間20分]

●バレリー、マット、ジャックの3人の会話を聞き、話題になっている二人（下記1.と2.）がどう描写されているか、英語でa. ～ d. にメモを取ってください。その後、それぞれの考えや行動について、自分に当てはまるものを選んでチェックを入れ、さらにその理由を考えてみましょう。音声は何度聞いてもかまいません。必要に応じて次ページの「単語のヘルプ」も参考にしましょう（解答例と訳はpp. 29-30）。

🎧 03 ⋯⋯⋯⋯⋯⋯⋯⋯⋯⋯⋯⋯⋯⋯⋯⋯⋯⋯⋯⋯⋯⋯⋯⋯⋯⋯⋯◆

1. Nyla
   a. her desk　＿＿＿＿＿＿＿＿＿＿＿＿＿＿＿＿＿＿＿＿
   b. Jack's opinion　＿＿＿＿＿＿＿＿＿＿＿＿＿＿＿＿＿＿
   c. Valerie's opinion　＿＿＿＿＿＿＿＿＿＿＿＿＿＿＿＿＿
   d. Nyla's neighbor's attitude　＿＿＿＿＿＿＿＿＿＿＿＿＿

Choose the sentence(s) true for you.
   ☐ I would like to work in a relaxing atmosphere like Nyla's.
   ☐ I wouldn't like to have nonwork items on and around my desk.
   ☐ I would complain if my neighbor were like Nyla.
   And why do you feel that way?

＿＿＿＿＿＿＿＿＿＿＿＿＿＿＿＿＿＿＿＿＿＿＿＿＿＿＿＿＿

2. a broker, Jack's friend
   a. his desk　＿＿＿＿＿＿＿＿＿＿＿＿＿＿＿＿＿＿＿＿＿＿
   b. Matt's opinion　＿＿＿＿＿＿＿＿＿＿＿＿＿＿＿＿＿＿＿
   c. Valerie's opinion　＿＿＿＿＿＿＿＿＿＿＿＿＿＿＿＿＿＿
   d. the broker's plans　＿＿＿＿＿＿＿＿＿＿＿＿＿＿＿＿＿

Choose the sentence(s) true for you.
   ☐ I would like to put pictures of my family on my desk.
   ☐ I would like to put more time into work and retire in my 30s or as

soon as possible.
- [ ] I would like to work regular hours and retire between the ages of 60 and 65.
And why do you feel that way?

(単語のヘルプ)

- [ ] disgusting　極めて不快な
- [ ] swear　誓う
- [ ] garden center　園芸店
- [ ] air plant　エアプランツ、土を必要としない着生植物
- [ ] hang out with 〜　（特に何をすることもなく）〜と一緒に過ごす
- [ ] overgrown　育ち過ぎた
- [ ] relaxed　（監視などが）緩い
- [ ] broker　株式仲買人、ブローカー
- [ ] get rid of 〜　〜を取り除く
- [ ] rake in　ぼろ儲けする
- [ ] devastate　破壊する
- [ ] ruin　ダメにする

2 以下のチャンクを聞き取るよう気を付けながら、もう一度、音声を聞きましょう。聞き取れたら □ にチェックを入れましょう。

🎧 **03** ....◆

☐ Hers isn't really a department I deal with　彼女の部署とはあまり付き合いはない

☐ I know what you're talking about.　何の話だかわかる

☐ super-disgusting or something　超汚いとか

☐ hanging from the wall　壁にぶら下げて

☐ hang out with her　（何をするでもなく）彼女と一緒にいる

☐ pops out between the leaves　葉の間からひょっこりと顔を出す

☐ make an excuse to go up there　口実を作ってそこに行く

☐ he'd have complained by now　これまでに文句を言っていただろう

☐ asked him to take it home　それを家に持ち帰るよう彼に言う

☐ nonwork items　仕事に関係ないもの

☐ doesn't seem to mind that much　そんなに気にしていないようだ

☐ devastate their health　健康をひどく損なう

☐ he's out entertaining clients　外に出かけて顧客を接待している

Unit
2

1. Nyla
   a. Her desk is surrounded by so many plants that it looks like she is working in a garden center or forest.
   b. She has too many plants around her desk.
   c. Her desk and its surroundings are relaxing.
   d. He hasn't complained so far, which means he has nothing against it.

Choose the sentence(s) true for you.
   ☐ I would like to work in a relaxing atmosphere like Nyla's. Because I would be able to concentrate on my work and be more productive in such an atmosphere.
   ☐ I wouldn't like to have nonwork items on and around my desk. Because I need a clean desk to be able to focus on my work.
   ☐ I would complain if my neighbor were like Nyla. Because I would have to do extra things like getting rid of fallen leaves from time to time.

日本語訳

1. ナイラ
a. 彼女の机の周りには植物が多過ぎて、園芸店か森の中で働いているように見える。
b. 彼女の机の周りには植物が多過ぎる。
c. 彼女の机やその周辺ではリラックスできる。
d. 彼はこれまで文句を言っていないので、そのことに何の反感も持っていないということだ。

あなたに当てはまる文を選びなさい。
☐ ナイラのようなリラックスできる環境で仕事がしたい。そうした環境にいれば、仕事に集中したり、生産性が上がったりするだろうから。
☐ 机の上や周りに仕事に関係のないものは置きたくない。なぜなら仕事に集中するにはきれいな机が必要だから。
☐ 隣の席の人がナイラのようだったら文句を言うだろう。なぜなら、時折落ち葉を片付けるなど、余計なことをしなければならないだろうから。

2. a broker, Jack's friend
   a. He once had a picture of his family on his desk but was told to remove it.
   b. He can't believe it. He doesn't understand why the picture should be taken away.

c. He should put a mug with his family's picture on it beause a coffee mug is allowed.

d. He is retiring at 36.

Choose the sentence(s) true for you.

☐ I would like to put pictures of my family on my desk. Because my family is very important to me and it would help to motivate me.

☐ I would like to put more time into work and retire in my 30s or as soon as possible. Because work is not everything for me. I would also like to do something else while I'm relatively young.

☐ I would like to work regular hours and retire between the ages of 60 and 65. Because if I worked too much and ruined my health, I wouldn't be able to enjoy life after retirement.

| 日本語訳 |

2. ブローカー、ジャックの友人

a. 彼はかつて机の上に家族の写真を置いていたが、片付けるよう言われた。

b. 彼はそのことが信じられない。その写真を片付けなければならない理由が理解できない。

c. コーヒーマグは置いていてもいいのだから、家族の写真が付いたマグを置けばいい。

d. 彼は36歳で引退する。

あなたに当てはまる文を選びなさい。

☐ 机の上に家族の写真を飾りたい。なぜなら家族は自分にとって非常に大切で、仕事のやる気を出す助けになるから。

☐ 勤務時間をもっと増やして、30代、またはできるだけ早い時期に退職したい。なぜなら自分にとって仕事が全てではなく、比較的若いうちにほかのこともしたいから。

☐ 通常の労働時間で働き、60～65歳の間に退職したい。なぜなら働き過ぎて身体を壊してしまったら、退職後の生活が楽しめないから。

3 聞き取りのコツ

会話に登場する、二人の人物の仕事における特徴的な行動を聞き取ります。

● 誇張表現を理解する

... Nyla has about a thousand plants.

実際に、机の周りに1000本もの植物があるわけではなく、about a thousand
で so many 程度の量を考えればよいでしょう。

Nyla has a great number of plants around her desk.

と言っただけでは驚きが足りないので、このように表現しているのです。

Her computer monitor kind of pops out between the leaves.

机の周りに観葉植物が多いことを、「コンピューターモニターが葉の間から飛び出
しているようだ」と表現しています。

Her desk/computer is surrounded by so many leaves.

と言うよりもはるかに相手に与える印象が強くなります。

Those guys just rake it in.

rake は名詞では「熊手」のこと。これを動詞として使った rake in は「お金を (熊
手でかき集めるように) 大量に稼ぐ」を意味します。

Those guys make so much money.

では言い表せない「がっぽり感」を伝えることができます。

some of those guys just devastate their health

devastate は「壊滅させる」という強い意味を持ちます。damage や harm より
もひどく、「身体をボロボロにする」と言いたかったので、あえてこの動詞を使って
います。

● I don't know. の意味

会話には何度か I don't know. が使われていますが、「私は知りません」では意味
が通じない場合があります。

Matt: I feel like I need to make an excuse to go up there now, just to
      see it.
Jack: I don't know.

ジャックはマットが言ったことについて、「そうかな」と懐疑的な気持ちを口にしてい
ます。

Matt: What does her neighbor think of it?
Valerie: I don't know.
これは「知りません」の意味です。

Valerie: You should … See if they make him get rid of that, too.
Jack: Ha-ha. I don't know, Valerie.
「よくわからないけど、どうなんだろうね」という気持ちです。

Matt: Wow. Brokers, right? Those guys just rake it in. We're in the wrong business.
Jack: I don't know. I mean, …
「それはどうだかわからないけど」と前置きし、実際に言いたいことはI mean（だって）のあとで述べられています。

 すぐに応用したい表現

super-disgusting or something
→ super-はいろいろな形容詞につけて、「とても」を表します。or something は「など」にあたる、幅を持たせた表現です。

up there
→直訳すると「上の階のあの場所に」。逆の down there もよく使われます。

those little air plants/a little picture of his family
→ little は「小さい」だけではなく、「大したことのない、ちょっとした」（前者）もしくは「かわいい」（後者）という感情を含んだ意味も持ちます。

kind of
→動詞などの前に置いて、「なんとなく」の意味を表します。

What a choice, though!
→この though は「だけれども」ではなく、She is talented!（彼女は才能があるね！）というコメントに対する Isn't it, though!（本当にそうですね）のように、「まったく、本当に」のニュアンスを付け加えます。

では英文を見ながら、もう一度、聞きましょう。

 03

Valerie: Hey, Matt, do you know Nyla — the content writer on the sixth floor?

Matt: I think I've spoken to her a couple of times in the kitchen. Hers isn't really a department I deal with, you know?

Valerie: Oh, man. You should see her desk!

Jack: Oh, I know what you're talking about, Valerie. Ha!

Matt: What, what? Is it, like, super-disgusting or something?

Jack: No, Matt, it's that Nyla has about a thousand plants. I swear, it's like a garden center up there. Seriously. They're on the desk, on the floor around her. She's got those little air plants hanging from the wall ...

Valerie: Well, she's got that sweet corner desk. I have to go up there pretty regularly, and it's so ... relaxing! I just want to hang out with her all day. It's like being in a forest. Her computer monitor kind of pops out between the leaves.

Matt: I feel like I need to make an excuse to go up there now, just to see it.

Jack: I don't know. It's too much for me. I just couldn't work like that. I need a clean desk.

Valerie: It's clean, Jack! It's just overgrown.

Matt: What does her neighbor think of it?

Valerie: I don't know. I've never really spoken to him. But I think if there was any problem, he'd have complained by now, wouldn't he?

Jack: Well, we're pretty lucky here. I think management is relaxed about that kind of thing. I've got a friend who's a broker. One time, he put a little picture of his family on his desk, and his supervisor asked him to take it home.

Matt: What!? You've got to be kidding, Jack. That's just laughable.

Jack: They told him there can't be any nonwork items on his desk, except a coffee mug or things like that. It's even in his contract.

Valerie: You should buy him one of those mugs with a picture of his family on it. See if they make him get rid of that, too.

Jack: Ha-ha. I don't know, Valerie. He doesn't seem to mind that much, but he plans on quitting soon anyway.

Matt: Moving to a new company?

Jack: No, retiring! Yeah, he's going to retire at 36, he says.

Matt: Wow. Brokers, right? Those guys just rake it in. We're in the wrong business.

Jack: I don't know. I mean, retiring at 36 sounds great, but some of those guys just devastate their health. I mean, he's at work from 5 a.m., and most of the time he's out entertaining clients at bars until 10 p.m. He's 34 and he looks more like he's 45.

Valerie: What a choice, though! Ruin your health but retire by 36, or work regular hours until you're 65.

Matt: Surrounded by houseplants.

Valerie: Ha-ha. Yeah.

日本語訳

バレリー：ねえ、マット、6階にいるコンテンツライターのナイラを知ってる？

マット：給湯室で2、3回彼女と話したことがあると思う。彼女の部署とはあまり付き合いはないけど。

バレリー：ほんとに？　彼女の机を見てよ！

ジャック：ああ、何の話かわかったよ、バレリー。ははは！

マット：何、何？　超汚いとか？

ジャック：そうじゃないよ、マット、あのナイラのことさ、彼女は1000本くらいの植物を育てているんだ。ほんと、あそこ、園芸店みたいだよ。マジで。机の上や周りの床に置いてある。壁によくある小さなエアプランツをぶら下げているし…。

バレリー：あのかわいいコーナーデスクの持ち主ね。私、そこに定期的に行かなければならないんだけど、とても…リラックスできるの！　ほんとに一日中彼女と一緒に過ごしたいわ。まるで森の中にいるみたい。彼女のコンピューターモニターは葉の間からひょっこり顔を出しているって感じ。

マット：今そこに行く用事を作りたい気分だよ、それを見るためだけに。

ジャック：そうかなあ。僕にはやり過ぎだな。ああいう風には働けないよ。机はきれいじゃなきゃ。

バレリー：きれいよ、ジャック。ただ…伸び過ぎているだけ。

マット：隣の人はどう思っているの？

バレリー：知らないわ。彼とはあまり話したことがないから。でも、もし何か問題があったら、これまでに文句を言っていたんじゃないかな、でしょ？

ジャック：まあ、僕たちはこの会社にいてラッキーだよ。経営陣はその種のことについて緩いからね。僕の友だちでブローカーをしているのがいるんだけどさ。あるとき、彼が自分の机の上に家族のいい感じの写真を置いたら、上司がそれを家に持って帰るように言ったんだ。

マット：え!?　冗談だろ、ジャック。くだらない。

ジャック：会社から、机の上にはコーヒーマグなんかを除いて、仕事に関係ないものはいっさい置いてはいけないって言われたんだ。彼の契約書にまでそう書いてある。

バレリー：彼の家族の写真がついているマグカップを買ってあげるべきね。会社がそれも彼に処分させるかどうか見たいものだわ。

ジャック：ははは。どうだろうね、バレリー。彼はそれほど気にしていないようだけど、いずれにせよ近いうちに辞めるつもりだし。

マット：新しい会社に移るの？

ジャック：いや、引退だよ!　そう、36歳で引退するって言ってる。

マット：すごい。証券会社勤めだよね。ぼろもうけの業界だから。僕たち、仕事の選択を間違えたよね。

ジャック：どうかな。だって、36歳で退職するって聞こえはいいけど、彼らの中には健康をひどく損なう人もいるから。実際、彼は午前5時から仕事をしていて、たいてい午後10時までバーで顧客の接待をしている。34歳だけど、どっちかというと45歳に見えるんだ。

バレリー：ほんと、まったく大した選択よね!　健康を損ねるけど36歳までに引退するか、65歳まで通常の労働時間で働くか。

マット：観葉植物に囲まれて。

バレリー：ははは。そうね。

ダイアログの内容について下記の設問に答えましょう。解答と解説、翻訳はページの下にあります。

Q1 What does Valerie mean when she says "I just want to hang out with her all day"?
(A) She feels comfortable surrounded by plants.
(B) She is going to work in a forest in the future.
(C) She would like to go up to her floor now.
(D) She needs to move her desk to a corner.

Q2 What is the broker going to do?
(A) He is moving to another company.
(B) He is entertaining his client at a bar.
(C) He is retiring at a very early age.
(D) He is moving his family's picture to some other place.

解答と解説

Q1 解答（A）
バレリーの言う「彼女と一日中一緒にいたい」とは、どういう意味ですか？
(A) 植物に囲まれていると心地よい。
(B) 将来は森の中で働きたい。
(C) いますぐ彼女がいる階に行きたい。
(D) 自分の机を角に移動させる必要がある。

解説 バレリーは、she's got that sweet corner desk の sweet（心地よい）と、it's so ... relaxing の relaxing（リラックスするような）で、植物に囲まれたナイラの机について肯定的な意見を述べています。そこで「一日中一緒にいたい」と言っているので、その環境にいると「心地よい」という(A)が正解です。

Q2 解答（C）
その証券会社の社員は、今後何をするつもりですか？
(A) 他の会社に移る。
(B) バーで顧客を接待する。
(C) 非常に若くして引退する。
(D) 家族の写真を別な場所に移動する。

解説 その友人であるジャックは、Moving to a new company? という質問に対して、No, retiring! と、また、... retire at 36 と答えています。この at 36 を at a very early age と言い換えた(C)が正解です。

6 最後に、スラッシュの箇所でリピートしてみます。かたまりごとに、意味が
わかっているか確認しながら口に出してみましょう。

🎧 04

Valerie: Hey, Matt, do you know Nyla / — the content writer on the sixth floor? //

Matt: I think I've spoken to her / a couple of times in the kitchen. // Hers isn't really a department I deal with, / you know? //

Valerie: Oh, man. // You should see her desk! //

Jack: Oh, I know what you're talking about, Valerie. // Ha! //

Matt: What, what? // Is it, like, super-disgusting or something? //

Jack: No, Matt, it's that Nyla has about a thousand plants. // I swear, / it's like a garden center up there. // Seriously. // They're on the desk, / on the floor around her. // She's got those little air plants / hanging from the wall ... //

Valerie: Well, she's got that sweet corner desk. // I have to go up there pretty regularly, / and it's so ... relaxing! // I just want to hang out with her / all day. // It's like being in a forest. // Her computer monitor kind of pops out / between the leaves. //

Matt: I feel like / I need to make an excuse to go up there now, / just to see it. //

Jack: I don't know. // It's too much for me. // I just couldn't work like that. // I need a clean desk. //

Valerie: It's clean, Jack! // It's just overgrown. //

Matt: What does her neighbor think of it? //

Valerie: I don't know. // I've never really spoken to him. // But I think if there was any problem, / he'd have complained by now, wouldn't he? //

Jack: Well, we're pretty lucky here. // I think management is relaxed / about that kind of thing. // I've got a friend who's a broker. // One time, he put a little picture of his family on his desk, / and his supervisor asked him to take it home. //

Matt: What!? // You've got to be kidding, Jack. // That's just laughable. //

Jack: They told him / there can't be any nonwork items on his desk, / except a coffee mug or things like that. // It's even in his contract. //

Valerie: You should buy him / one of those mugs with a picture of his family on it. // See if they make him get rid of that, too. //

Jack: Ha-ha. // I don't know, Valerie. // He doesn't seem to mind that much, / but he plans on quitting soon anyway. //

Matt: Moving to a new company? //

Jack: No, retiring! // Yeah, he's going to retire at 36, he says. //

Matt: Wow. // Brokers, right? // Those guys just rake it in. // We're in the wrong business. //

Jack: I don't know. // I mean, retiring at 36 sounds great, / but some of those guys just devastate their health. / I mean, he's at work from 5 a.m., / and most of the time / he's out entertaining clients at bars until 10 p.m. // He's 34 and he looks more like he's 45. //

Valerie: What a choice, though! // Ruin your health but retire by 36, / or work regular hours until you're 65. //

Matt: Surrounded by houseplants. //

Unit
2

Valerie: Ha-ha. // Yeah. //

🎧 05-06　　　　　　　　　　　　　　　　　　　**LISTENING**

難易度 ●●● ○ ○ 3　｜約450語（やや長い）｜日常／夫婦の会話　🇺🇸 女　🇺🇸 男

TASK

1 あなたは配偶者を含む同居者と家事の分担表を作ることにしました。それぞれの仕事や学業などを勘案し、効率的で公平感のある一覧表を作成しましょう。　　　　　　　　[学習目標時間20分]

● 音声を聞き、夫婦それぞれが行なっていることを①Table A の各欄にチェック☑をつけてください。②その後、あなた自身のことについて Table B の家事分担一覧表（Household Chore List）の各カテゴリーの what の欄に具体的な作業を、who と how often の欄には担当する人と頻度を記入しましょう。必要に応じて次ページの「単語のヘルプ」も参考にしましょう（解答例は pp. 43-44）。

🎧 05 ･･ ◆

① Table A

	work	cooking	lawn mowing	cleaning	doing laundry
wife					
husband					

② Table B (Household Chore List)

CATEGORIES	what	who	how often
cleaning			
dining			
doing laundry			
child rearing			
taking care of the garden			
taking care of the pets			

Unit
3

> 単語のヘルプ

- ☐ do overtime　残業する
- ☐ swim meet　水泳大会
- ☐ drop one's stuff　（帰宅して）荷物を置く
- ☐ heat　予選の一試合
- ☐ sweaty　汗にまみれた
- ☐ expect 〜　〜が来るのを期待する
- ☐ devastated　落ち込んでいる
- ☐ It's not like ...　…というわけではない
- ☐ exhausted　ひどく疲れている
- ☐ imply　ほのめかす
- ☐ sprawl oneself out　寝そべる
- ☐ a load of laundry　洗濯1回分
- ☐ could use 〜　〜があるといい
- ☐ parental　親の
- ☐ move one's butt　行動を起こす、腰を上げる

2 以下のチャンクを聞き取るよう気を付けながら、もう一度、音声を聞きましょう。聞き取れたら □ にチェックを入れましょう。

🎧 05 ⋯⋯⋯⋯⋯⋯⋯⋯⋯⋯⋯⋯⋯⋯⋯⋯⋯⋯⋯⋯⋯⋯⋯⋯⋯⋯⋯⋯⋯⋯◆

☐ managed to get out of it　それを何とかして回避した

☐ There's no time for that.　それをしている時間はない。

☐ get myself something to eat　自分で食事の用意をする

☐ You're unbelievable.　信じられないわ（何ていうことを言っているの）。

☐ it's just this once　今回だけだよ

☐ Can we not do this right now?　今はこんなことするのはやめないか？

☐ expect me to cook dinner　私が夕食を準備することを期待する

☐ make it look effortless　難なくやっているように見せる

☐ When was the last time ...?　最後に…したのはいつだった？

☐ getting away from the point　話がずれてきている

☐ The point is that ...　重要なのは…ということだ。

☐ it wouldn't make any difference　そうした／そうであったとしても同じことだろう

TASK の解答例

Table A

	work	cooking	lawn mowing	cleaning	doing laundry
wife	✓	✓		✓	✓
husband	✓	✓ (but not much)	✓		

Table B (Household Chore List)

以下は what 欄に入る作業例です。who の欄にはそれぞれの家事を担当する人のイニシャルを、how often の欄には every day、once a week/month などの頻度を入れます。該当しない項目については、who と how often の欄に×を書きましょう。

CATEGORIES	what	who	how often
cleaning [掃除]	Clean rooms　部屋の掃除		
	Dust　ホコリ取り		
	Mop floors　モップがけ		
	Sweep　拭き掃除		
	Vacuum　掃除機がけ		
	Put things in their place　片付け		
	Take out the trash　ゴミ出し		
dining [食事]	Do grocery shopping　食料品の買い出し		
	Prepare meals　料理のしたく		
	Wash dishes　皿洗い		
doing laundry [洗濯]	Separate the clothes　洗濯物を仕分ける		
	Hang the laundry　洗濯物を干す		
	Take in the laundry　洗濯物を取り込む		
	Fold and put away the laundry　洗濯物を畳んでしまう		
child rearing [子育て]	Send them to school　学校へ送る		
	Collect them from school　学校に迎えにいく		
	Go out with them on holidays　休日に一緒に出かける		
	Help them with schoolwork　宿題を手伝う		

	Feed them　食事を与える		
	Put them to sleep　寝かしつける		
	Changing diapers　おむつを替える		
taking care of the garden/plants [庭や植物の手入れ]	Mow the lawn　芝を刈る		
	Water plants　植物に水をやる		
	Weed the garden　庭の雑草を取る		
taking care of the pets [ペットの世話]	Feed pets　ペットに餌をやる		
	Walk the dog　犬を散歩させる		
	Clean the cage　ケージを掃除する		

③ 聞き取りのコツ

普段から会話を交わしている二人である点、および、途中言い合いになっている点に気をつけて聞きましょう。

● **意味の取り違いに気をつける**

同じ表現でも、その状況で使われているからこそその意味があります。表面的にとらえて誤解しないように気をつけましょう。

Why are you home?

×「なぜ家にいるの?」

この後に I thought you were doing overtime tonight? と言っていることから、

○「もう帰ってきたの?」

という意味だとわかります。

You look fine.

×「あなた、元気そうね」

夫の I really need to have a shower and change. への応答として、

○「(着替えたりしないでも) 見た感じ、大丈夫よ」

と言っています。

Why don't you just go?

×「単に行ったら?」

夫が妻だけ行けばいいのにと言っている文脈なので、この just は go ではなく you にかかり、

○「君だけ行ったら?」

の意味だとわかります。

Really?

×「ほんとなの?」

妻が When was the last time you even did a load of laundry? と言うと、夫がすかさず When was the last time you mowed the lawn? と質問をかぶせます。よくある反論のパターンですが、それを聞いた妻が発した言葉なので、

○「それ、本気で言ってるの?」

ととらえたほうがより適切です。

● 何が省略されているかを判断する

文脈から何が省略されているかを正確に把握する必要があります。

..., but it isn't.

この前にI make it look effortless (努力を要しないように見せている) と言って
いることから、it isn'tの後にはeffortlessが省略されているとわかります。主語
が変わっているので注意が必要です。

We can and we will.

夫のWe can discuss all that other stuff later.に対する応答なので、canと
willの後にはdiscuss all that other stuff laterが省略されています。同じcan
だけで答えるのではなく、「そうしましょう」の意味でwillと付け加えている点にも
注目しましょう。

 すぐに応用したい表現

You're unbelievable. (すごい／信じられない)
→会話では「あなた、何を言っているの？」と悪い意味で使われていますが、「(相
手の業績・言動・能力などが) すばらしい」という良い意味でも使われます。

You're implying it. (そう言いたいんでしょ)
→直訳すると、「あなたはそう暗示している」。言葉の裏の意味を推し量ったとき
の表現です。

When was the last time ...? (最後に…したのはいつでしたか？)
→lastをfirstにすれば、何かを最初に経験したときを尋ねる表現になります。

I could just use a little help. (ちょっと助けてもらえるとうれしいんだけど)
→could useのあとには抽象的なことだけでなく、a glass of waterなどを続け
ることもできます。「水を1杯もらえるとうれしい」という意味です。

4 では英文を見ながら、もう一度、聞きましょう。

🎧 05

Wife: Oh, hi! Why are you home? I thought you were doing overtime tonight.

Husband: Hi, honey. Yeah, I managed to get out of it.

W: Great, so you can come with me to Kylie's swim meet! She'll be so happy. Just drop your stuff and let's go.

H: Uh, I really need to have a shower and change.

W: There's no time for that. We have to go now. It starts at 5:30, and she's in the first heat. You look fine.

H: Hon, it's been a really busy day, and I'm hot and sweaty. Why don't you just go? I'll get myself something to eat. She wasn't expecting me anyway.

W: You're unbelievable. Come on, Ben. You know how devastated she was when I told her you weren't going.

H: I've been to dozens of her meets. It's not like it's her first time or something.

W: No, but if she does well at this one, she could qualify for the state championships.

H: Sure. And there's always another level, another competition. Look, it's just this once. I'm exhausted.

W: How do you think I feel? I just got back from work, too, Ben. Do you think I work less than you?

H: I didn't say that.

W: You're implying it.

H: Can we not do this right now?

W: I think it's time we talked about this story that you work so hard. Yes, Ben, you work hard. But so do I. And when you come home, you put your bags down, take a shower and sprawl yourself out on the couch. But you still expect me to cook dinner for all of us and keep the house clean. I mean, maybe I make it look effortless, but it isn't.

H: Hey, I cook, too.

W: Oh, right. Yes, you make spaghetti and meat sauce every other week. When was the last time you even did a load of laundry?

H: When was the last time you mowed the lawn?

W: Really? You mow the lawn once a week at most. I do laundry almost every day, Ben. I could just use a little help here once in a while. Anyway, you're getting away from the point. The point is that we've both got responsibilities, and many of them are parental. This swim meet is really important to Kylie.

H: I know. I just thought that since I was supposed to work late anyway, it wouldn't make any difference. But you're right. I'm sorry. Kylie will be happier to see us both there. I don't want to disappoint her. We can discuss all that other stuff later.

W: We can and we will. Now, move your butt. Let's go!

日本語訳

妻：あら！ なぜ家にいるの？ 今夜は残業かと思っていたわ。

夫：やあ、ハニー。ああ、何とかそうならずにすんだんだ。

妻：よかった、じゃあ、カイリーの水泳大会に一緒に来られるわね！ あの子、とても喜ぶわよ。荷物を置いて、行きましょう。

夫：えーと、シャワーを浴びて着替えないと。

妻：そんな時間はないわ。もう行かないと。5時30分に大会が始まって、あの子は最初のレースに出るから。そのままで大丈夫よ。

夫：ねえ、すごく忙しい一日で、暑くて汗びっしょりなんだ。君だけ行ってきたら？ 僕は自分で食事の用意をするよ。そもそもカイリーは僕が来るとは思っていなかったことだし。

妻：信じられないわ。さあ、ベン。あなたが行けないと話したとき、あの子がどれだけ落ち込んでいたか知っているでしょう。

夫：出場した大会には何十回も行ってるよ。あの子にとって初めてってわけでもないんだから。

妻：初めてじゃないけど、もしこの大会でいい成績を残せば、州大会の出場資格が得られるかもしれないの。

夫：そうだね。それにまた、別のレベル、別の大会があるんだよね。ね、今回だけだよ。くたくたなんだ。

妻：私の気持ちはどうなの？ 私も仕事から戻ったばかりよ、ベン。私はあなたより仕事していない

と思っているの？

夫：そんなこと言ってない。

妻：ほのめかしてるわ。

夫：今はこの話はやめようよ。

妻：あなたが一生懸命働いているということについて、今、話すべきね。ええ、ベン、あなたはよく働いているわ。でも、私もそう。そして、あなたは家に帰ってきたら、バッグを置いて、シャワーを浴びて、ソファーに寝そべってる。でもあなたは、私がみんなのために夕食を作って、家をきれいにしておくことを期待している。難なくやっているように見せているかもしれないけど、実際はそうじゃないのよ。

夫：ねえ、僕も料理をするよ。

妻：ああ、そうね。ええ、スパゲッティ・ミートソースは1週間おきに作っているわ。最後に洗濯をしたのはいつ？

夫：君が最後に芝を刈ったのはいつだ？

妻：本気で聞いているの？　あなたが芝生を刈るのはせいぜい週に1回。私はほとんど毎日洗濯をしているわよ、ベン。たまに手伝ってくれれば助かるのよ。とにかく、あなたの話はポイントがずれてきている。重要なのは、私たち二人とも責任があり、その多くは親としての責任だということ。この水泳大会は、カイリーにとって本当に重要なのよ。

夫：わかってる。もともと遅くまで仕事をすることになっていたから、（行かなくても）同じことだと思っていたんだ。でも君の言うとおりだよ。ごめん。僕たちが二人で行ったほうがカイリーは喜ぶよね。彼女を失望させたくない。ほかのことはあとで話し合おう。

妻：後回しにできるし、あとで必ず話しましょう。さあ、身体を動かして。行きましょう！

Unit **3**

5 ダイアログの内容について下記の設問に答えましょう。解答と解説、翻訳はページの下にあります。

Q1 Which statement is true about Kylie?
　　(A) She is going to have a shower and take part in the swim meet.
　　(B) She wants her parents to come to see her competition.
　　(C) She is seen as a candidate for a national champion.
　　(D) She is disappointed because she was defeated in the race.

Q2 How often does the man mow the lawn?
　　(A) Every other day
　　(B) Every other week
　　(C) Once a week at most
　　(D) Once a month at most

解答と解説

Q1 解答（B）
カイリーについて正しい記述はどれですか?
(A) シャワーを浴びてから水泳大会に参加する。
(B) 両親に競技会を見に来てほしいと思っている。
(C) 国内チャンピオンになると見られている。
(D) レースで負けたのでがっかりしている。

解説 カイリーの水泳大会について話している中で、妻の how devastated she was when I told her you weren't going（あなたが行けないと話したときにいかに落ち込んだか）や夫の Kylie will be happier to see us both there.（僕たちが二人で行ったほうがカイリーは喜ぶよね）から、カイリーは両親に見に来てほしいと考えていることがわかるので、正解は(B)です。

Q2 解答（C）
夫はどのぐらいの頻度で芝刈りをしますか?
(A) 1日おきに
(B) 隔週に
(C) 多くて週1回
(D) 多くて月1回

解説 When was the last time you mowed the lawn?（君が最後に芝を刈ったのはいつだ?）と聞かれた妻が、You mow the lawn once a week at most.（あなたが芝刈りをするのはせいぜい週1回よ）と言って、「そんなこと聞くけど、私はほぼ毎日洗濯してるわ」と反撃しています。ここから、(C)が正解だとわかります。

> **6** 最後に、スラッシュの箇所でリピートしてみます。かたまりごとに、意味が
> わかっているか確認しながら口に出してみましょう。

🎧 **06** ··◆

Wife: Oh, hi! // Why are you home? // I thought you were doing overtime tonight. //

Husband: Hi, honey. // Yeah, I managed to get out of it. //

W: Great, / so you can come with me / to Kylie's swim meet! // She'll be so happy. // Just drop your stuff and let's go. //

H: Uh, I really need to have a shower and change. //

W: There's no time for that. // We have to go now. // It starts at 5:30, / and she's in the first heat. // You look fine. //

H: Hon, it's been a really busy day, / and I'm hot and sweaty. // Why don't you just go? // I'll get myself something to eat. // She wasn't expecting me anyway. //

W: You're unbelievable. // Come on, Ben. // You know how devastated she was / when I told her you weren't going. //

H: I've been to dozens of her meets. // It's not like / it's her first time or something. //

W: No, but if she does well at this one, / she could qualify for the state championships. //

H: Sure. // And there's always another level, / another competition. / Look, it's just this once. // I'm exhausted. //

W: How do you think I feel? // I just got back from work, too, Ben. //

51

Do you think I work less than you? //

H: I didn't say that. //

W: You're implying it. //

H: Can we not do this right now? //

W: I think it's time we talked about this story / that you work so hard.
// Yes, Ben, you work hard. // But so do I. // And when you come
home, / you put your bags down, / take a shower / and sprawl
yourself out on the couch. // But you still expect me to cook dinner
for all of us / and keep the house clean. // I mean, / maybe I make it
look effortless, / but it isn't. //

H: Hey, I cook, too. //

W: Oh, right. // Yes, you make spaghetti and meat sauce / every other
week. // When was the last time / you even did a load of laundry? //

H: When was the last time / you mowed the lawn? //

W: Really? // You mow the lawn once a week at most. // I do laundry
almost every day, Ben. // I could just use a little help here / once in
a while. // Anyway, you're getting away from the point. // The point
is that / we've both got responsibilities, / and many of them are
parental. // This swim meet is really important to Kylie. //

H: I know. // I just thought that / since I was supposed to work late
anyway, / it wouldn't make any difference. // But you're right. // I'm
sorry. // Kylie will be happier to see us both there. // I don't want to
disappoint her. // We can discuss all that other stuff later. //

W: We can and we will. // Now, move your butt. // Let's go! //

一件落着。

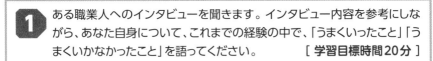

🎧 07-09 **LISTENING**

難易度 ●●● 3 | 約460語（やや長い） | 技術／インタビュー | 🇺🇸 女 🇺🇸 男

TASK

1 ある職業人へのインタビューを聞きます。インタビュー内容を参考にしながら、あなた自身について、これまでの経験の中で、「うまくいったこと」「うまくいかなかったこと」を語ってください。 [学習目標時間20分]

● 音声を聞いて以下の①②について考えてみましょう。必要に応じて次ページの「単語のヘルプ」も参考にしましょう（解答例は pp. 57-58）。

🎧 07 ....◆

①インタビューから、これまでの経験を語る際に使える表現を聞き取り、以下の枠内に書きましょう。

②次の一覧から自分の経験に当てはまる言い方を選び、①の表現も使いながら自分の経験を英語で語りましょう。

	うまくいったこと	うまくいかなかったこと
school	make many friends	can't make friends
	enter a name school	fail an extrance exam
	get all As	flunk a course
	was praised a lot by	be scolded
	win a prize	be defeated by an opponent

work	get a promotion	be fired or lose a job
	get a pay raise	take a pay cut
	change jobs successfully	be out of work
	open a business	lose a business
	have good colleagues	feel lonely at work
private life	get a boyfriend/girlfriend	break up with your love
	get married	get divorced
	buy a house	have to sell the house
	recover from an illness	suffer from an illness
	take a trip abroad	get sick while traveling

Unit
4

[My Experiences]

(単語のヘルプ)

☐ blacksmithing　鍛冶　＊blacksmith は「鍛冶職人」の意味。

☐ perspective　視点

☐ idly　ぼんやりと、だらだらと

☐ intricate　（作りが）複雑な

☐ look into 〜　〜を調べる

☐ flexibility　柔軟性

☐ durability　耐久性

☐ property　特性、性質

☐ go the other way　逆方向に行く

☐ refined　洗練された

☐ recognize　（本人だと）認識する

☐ cleaver　（肉用の）大包丁

☐ splinter　バラバラになる

☐ thrilled　感激している

以下のチャンクを聞き取るよう気を付けながら、もう一度、音声を聞きましょう。聞き取れたら □ にチェックを入れましょう。

🎧 07

☐ what brought you to blacksmithing　あなたが鍛冶を始めた理由

☐ from a historical perspective　歴史的な視点から

☐ remember watching a film　ある映画を見たことを覚えている

☐ much more scientific than ...　…よりもずっと科学的な

☐ quite a bit　かなり

☐ feel like a natural fit　しっくりくる

☐ started working toward that goal　その目標に向けて取り組み始めた

☐ get orders from all over the world　世界中から注文を受けている

☐ willing to pay a little more for ...　…にもう少し (お金を) 出してもいいと思う

☐ it turned out to be extremely challenging　極めて大変だということがわかった

☐ in the end　最終的には

TASKの解答例

① When I started, I was coming at...（始めたとき…から取り掛かりました）
I remember ...ing（…したのを覚えています）
I started ...ing（…し始めました）
mostly I started with...（だいたいは…から始めました）
the more ..., the more ...（…すればするほど…です）

② 会話や表現一覧を参考にし、p. 58のような英文が作れればいいでしょう。

p. 58

	うまくいったこと	うまくいかなかったこと
school 学校	make many friends 多くの友だちを作る	can't make friends 友だちができない
	enter a name school 有名校に入る	fail an extrance exam 受験に失敗する
	get all As オール5を取る	flunk a course 単位を落とす
	was praised a lot by 褒められる	be scolded 怒られる
	win a prize 賞をもらう	be defeated by an opponent 競争相手に負ける
work 仕事	get a promotion 昇進する	be fired or lose a job 解雇されるか失業する
	get a pay raise 昇給する	take a pay cut 減給になる
	change jobs successfully 転職に成功する	be out of work 無職になる
	open a business 店を開店させる	lose a business 商売で失敗する
	have good colleagues いい同僚を持つ	feel lonely at work 職場で孤立する
private life 私生活	get a boyfriend/girlfriend 彼氏／彼女ができる	break up with your love 恋人と別れる
	get married 結婚する	get divorced 離婚する
	buy a house 家を買う	have to sell the house 家を売却せざるをえなくなる
	recover from an illness 病気が治る	suffer from an illness 病気になる
	take a trip abroad 海外旅行をする	get sick while traveling 旅先で病気になる

Unit **4**

【My Experiences】

I was a very good student. When I was in the third year of high school, I got all As and received a lot of praise from my favorite teacher. After graduating from one of the top colleges, I started my career as a junior high school teacher. I had great colleagues and had a great time at work. I remember preparing for my classes until midnight almost every day. The more I put in hours, the better, I thought. But one day, my life changed. I suffered from a serious illness and was hospitalized. Luckily, I went back to a normal life after a while. Now I'm spending more time on my hobbies than on my work.

| 日本語訳 |

私は学生時代、とても優秀でした。高校3年生の時、オール5を取って大好きな先生に褒められました。難関大学を卒業後、中学校教師として働きはじめました。すばらしい同僚もいて、楽しい職場でした。ほぼ毎日、深夜0時まで授業の準備をしていたことを覚えています。(仕事には)時間をかければかけるほどよい、と思っていました。しかしある日、人生が変わりました。重い病気にかかり、入院したのです。幸いなことに、しばらくして普通の生活に戻れました。いまは仕事よりも趣味に時間を割いています。

🎧 08

確認のために My Experiences の音声を聞いてみましょう。

3 聞き取りのコツ

インタビュアーは簡潔にかつ話の流れに沿って質問をし、答える側は伝えたい内容をどのように展開させていくかを考えることが大事です。

● **質問の仕方**

音声では、

So, let's begin with ... (まず…から始めましょう)

So you wanted ... (wondering, "How ... make such intricate swords and knives?" に対して)

So, did you cook quite a bit? (the more I kept reading ... kitchen knives. に対して)

So, who are your clients now? (新たな側面からの質問として)

Do clients ever request ...? (顧客の話を膨らませるために)

のように、話の流れを拾って次への展開に結びつけています。

Unit
4

● **時系列に沿って答える**

時間の経過に沿って話を進めると相手にもわかりやすくなります。レイトマンさんの最初の発言だけを見ても、

originally (もともとは)

When I started... (始めたころは)

So (そこで)

と、ところどころに時に関する表現を使って、流れを明確にしていることがわかります。

● **質問に対して Yes/No で答えたとき**

単に Yes. や No. と答えるだけでなく、それに関連する詳細情報を付け加えています。その際、

actually (実際には)

the thing is ... (実は、肝心なのは)

I wanted ... (本当は…したかった)

I realized ... ([しかし、それで] …だとわかった)

などの表現の続きには、より大切な内容が述べられることが多いので、注意して聞きましょう。

● 例示する

例を挙げると話がわかりやすくなります。ここでは、for example を連発するのではなく、

mostly A although B（だいたいは A ですが B でもあります）

just last week, ...（ちょうど先週のことですが…）

I did have one person ...（…のような人がいました）

と、様々な言い回しで具体例を導入しています。

 すぐに応用したい表現

What brought you to ...?
→直訳すれば、「何があなたを…に持ってきたか」ですが、実際には理由を聞いている表現です。What brought you to Japan?（来日の目的は？）のようにも使えます。

Some are ..., some are ...
→「一部は…で、一部は…だ」のように全体の中の構成要素を表す言い方です。もちろん、be 動詞の代わりに一般動詞も使えます。Some are ..., others are ...とすることもできます。

It went the other way.
→「もう一方の方向に行った」、つまり、「まったく逆の結果になった」と言いたいときに使えます。

There's only so much you can do.
→so muchとありますが、たくさんあるわけではなく、「できることには限りがある」という意味です。

では英文を見ながら、もう一度、聞きましょう。

🎧 07

Interviewer: So, let's begin with what brought you to blacksmithing. Why did you want to begin making kitchen knives?

Reitman: Well, originally, it wasn't kitchen knives. When I started, I was coming at blacksmithing from a historical perspective. I remember watching a film that took place in the Middle Ages and just idly wondering, "How did these people, who didn't have electricity or power tools, manage to make such intricate swords and knives?" So I started looking into that.

Interviewer: Wow. So you wanted to make swords?

Reitman: Yes. And I actually did make a few swords. Some were good, some were really bad. But mostly I started with knives. The thing is, the more I worked at making better and better weapons, the more interested I became in the different qualities of steel — its flexibility, its durability. The carbon levels, the mix of other elements. It was much more scientific than I'd imagined. And the more I studied, the more I kept reading about the properties of delicate cutting tools like kitchen knives.

Interviewer: So, did you cook quite a bit? Did that feel like a natural fit?

Reitman: No, actually, it went the other way. I really wanted to make something that was refined. Really durable but fine. I realized that creating an excellent cooking knife would be the best test of my abilities as a blacksmith. And when I started working toward that goal, I actually started cooking more.

Interviewer: So, who are your clients now?

Reitman: I get orders from all over the world. Mostly from chefs, although occasionally they come from home cooks who are willing to pay a little more for a really fine knife. Just last week, I received an order for a set of five knives from a well-known television chef. I don't want to say his name, but you'd recognize him, I'm sure.

Interviewer: Do clients ever request anything unusual? Or do they leave the design mostly up to you?

Reitman: Luckily, most people are pretty respectful of the craft. I can't say I've had any truly strange requests. They will specify the size — the length and weight, for example. I might have to tell them if it's just not possible, like a meat cleaver that's super light. I mean, there's only so much you can do. I did have one person ask that I make a knife with a very specific rare wood as the handle. She ordered the wood for it herself, and it turned out to be extremely challenging to work with because it would splinter quite easily. But in the end, the knife was beautiful.

Interviewer: Another happy customer?

Reitman: I think I was as thrilled as she was, to be honest.

日本語訳

インタビュアー:まず、鍛冶を職業とされた理由から始めましょう。どうして包丁を作り始めたいと思われたのですか?

レイトマン:もともと(興味があったの)は包丁ではありませんでした。始めたころは歴史的な視点から鍛冶と向き合っていました。中世を舞台にした映画を見て、「電気も電動工具もなかったあの時代の人たちが、どうやってこのように手の込んだ刀やナイフを作ることができたのだろうか」とぼんやり考えていたのを覚えています。そこでそのことを調べ始めました。

インタビュアー:そうですか。ということは、刀をお作りになりたかったのですか?

レイトマン:はい。実際に刀を何本か作りました。出来がよいものもあれば、かなりひどいものもありました。でも主にナイフから作り始めました。実は、より優れた武器を作ろうとすればするほど、鋼鉄のさまざまな性質、つまり柔軟性や耐久性に興味を持つようになりました。炭素含有率、他の元素の混合といったことです。想像していたよりもずっと科学的でした。そして、研究すればするほど、包丁のような繊細な刃物の性質についての書物を読み続けていったのです。

インタビュアー:では、かなり料理をされたのですか。しっくりした感覚はありましたか?

レイトマン:いいえ、実はその逆でした。私は本当に洗練されたものを作りたいと思っていました。耐久性に優れ、それでいて繊細なものです。私は、優れた包丁を作ることが、鍛冶職人としての私の能力を最も正しく評価するものであると気づきました。そしてその目標に向けて取り組み始めたときになって、私は実際により多くの料理を作り始めたのです。

インタビュアー:今の顧客はどういった方々なのですか?

レイトマン:世界中から注文を受けています。ほとんどはシェフの方々からですが、時には、本当に

素晴らしい包丁にならもう少し（お金を）払ってもいいと思っている家庭でお料理をされている方からのご注文もあります。つい先週、テレビに出ている有名なシェフから包丁5本セットの注文を受けました。お名前は伏せておきたいのですが、聞けば必ず誰だかおわかりになるような方です。

インタビュアー：顧客が通常とは異なるものを要求することはあるのですか？　それともデザインはほぼあなたにお任せするのでしょうか？

レイトマン：幸いなことに、ほとんどの方々はこの手仕事をかなり尊重してくださいます。これまで本当に変わった要望があったというわけではありません。たとえば長さや重さといったサイズの指定はあります。超軽量の肉切り包丁（のご要望）といったように、それが可能ではないかどうかだけはお伝えしなければならない場合もあります。つまり、できることは限られているのです。私はある方から、ある特定の珍しい木材を柄にした包丁を作ってほしいと頼まれました。その方はご自分で（その包丁に使う）木材を注文されましたが、すぐに割れてしまうので、それを材料とするのは極めて難しいということがわかりました。しかし、最終的に、その包丁はきれいな出来となりました。

インタビュアー：またお一人、お客様を満足させたのですね？

レイトマン：正直なところ、私は彼女と同じくらい感激していたと思います。

Unit
4

ダイアログの内容について下記の設問に答えましょう。解答と解説、翻訳はページの下にあります。

Q1 What made the speaker interested in blacksmithing in the first place?
(A) Kitchen knives that famous chefs use
(B) Power tools in the Middle Ages
(C) Meat cleavers that are super light
(D) Swords and knives in a movie

Q2 Who are mentioned as the speaker's clients?
(A) Professional cooks
(B) Filmmakers
(C) Blacksmiths
(D) Woodcutters

解答と解説

Q1 解答（D）
話し手が最初に鍛冶に興味を持ったきっかけは何でしたか？
(A) 有名シェフらが使っている包丁
(B) 中世の動力工具
(C) 超軽量の肉切り包丁
(D) 映画に出ていた刀やナイフ

解説 最初に鍛冶に興味を持った理由を聞かれた話し手は、I remember watching a film that ... と、ある映画を見たことを挙げ、その中で How did ... manage to make such intricate swords and knives? という疑問が湧いたと言っているので、正解は (D) です。

Q2 解答（A）
話し手の顧客として述べられているのはだれですか？
(A) プロの料理人
(B) 映画製作者
(C) 鍛冶職人
(D) 木こり

解説 who are your clients now? と顧客について聞かれた話し手は、注文が来るのは Mostly from chefs と答えているので、(A) の professional cooks が正解だとわかります。

> **6** 最後に、スラッシュの箇所でリピートしてみます。かたまりごとに、意味が
> わかっているか確認しながら口に出してみましょう。

🎧 09 ·· ◆

Interviewer: So, let's begin with what brought you to blacksmithing. //
Why did you want to begin making kitchen knives? //

Reitman: Well, originally, / it wasn't kitchen knives. // When I started,
/ I was coming at blacksmithing from a historical perspective. // I
remember watching a film / that took place in the Middle Ages / and
just idly wondering, / "How did these people, / who didn't have
electricity or power tools, / manage to make such intricate swords
and knives?" // So I started looking into that. //

Interviewer: Wow. // So you wanted to make swords? //

Reitman: Yes. // And I actually did make a few swords. // Some were
good, some were really bad. // But mostly I started with knives. //
The thing is, / the more I worked at making better and better
weapons, / the more interested I became in the different qualities of
steel / — its flexibility, its durability. // The carbon levels, / the mix
of other elements. // It was much more scientific / than I'd imagined.
// And the more I studied, / the more I kept reading about the
properties / of delicate cutting tools like kitchen knives. //

Interviewer: So, did you cook quite a bit? // Did that feel like a natural
fit? //

Reitman: No, actually, it went the other way. // I really wanted to make
something / that was refined. // Really durable but fine. // I realized
that / creating an excellent cooking knife / would be the best test of
my abilities as a blacksmith. // And when I started working toward
that goal, / I actually started cooking more. //

Interviewer: So, who are your clients now? //

Reitman: I get orders from all over the world. // Mostly from chefs, / although occasionally they come from home cooks / who are willing to pay a little more / for a really fine knife. // Just last week, / I received an order for a set of five knives / from a well-known television chef. // I don't want to say his name, / but you'd recognize him, I'm sure. //

Interviewer: Do clients ever request anything unusual? // Or do they leave the design mostly up to you? //

Reitman: Luckily, most people are pretty respectful of the craft. // I can't say / I've had any truly strange requests. // They will specify the size / — the length and weight, for example. // I might have to tell them / if it's just not possible, / like a meat cleaver that's super light. // I mean, there's only so much you can do. // I did have one person ask that / I make a knife / with a very specific rare wood as the handle. // She ordered the wood for it herself, / and it turned out to be extremely challenging to work with / because it would splinter quite easily. // But in the end, / the knife was beautiful. //

Interviewer: Another happy customer? //

Reitman: I think I was as thrilled as she was, / to be honest. //

Unit
4

whitesmith は
「ブリキ職人」の意味です！

LISTENING

| 難易度 ●●●●● 3 | 450語（やや長い） | 新規ビジネス／インタビュー | 女 男 |

TASK

1 あなたは起業家にインタビューしています。提供されるサービスの長所を
より詳しく聞き出しましょう。　　　　[**学習目標時間20分**]

● 音声を繰り返し聞いて、以下の点についてメモを取りましょう。さらに、他社との
違いに関する追加の質問、および、想定される応答も考えてみましょう。必要に応
じて次ページの「単語のヘルプ」も参考にしましょう（解答例は pp. 71-72）。

🎧 10 ┄┄◆

メモを取るポイント

1. What is AliveHouse?

2. What are they working with?

3. What do they bring into a home?

4. What can you see at the end of the installation?

5. Why did the owner start the business?

6. What was the owner trained as?

7. What did the potted plants he worked on look like?

8. What was the owner's wife learning?

9. How did the owner and his wife work together?

10. What does the owner say about the price?

追加の質問：_____

応答：_____

追加の質問：_____

応答：_____

追加の質問：_____

応答：_____

（ 単語のヘルプ ）

☐ core 核となる

☐ integration 統合

☐ break down 分解する、細かく説明する

☐ sprinkle ちりばめる、点在させる

☐ comprehensive 総合的な

☐ tidy 整然とした

☐ take on （仕事などを）引き受ける

☐ installation 設置

☐ end up with 〜 最終的に〜になる

☐ be meant to 〜 （もともと）〜することになっている

☐ primal 原始的な

☐ fine-tuning 微調整

🎧 **10** ··· ◆

☐ Tell me a little about ...　…について少し教えてください。

☐ in the easiest way possible　できるかぎり簡単な方法で

☐ There are many, many different ways that ...　…するには実にたくさんの方法があります。

☐ the only things you see are ...　目にするものは…だけです。

☐ a problem to be solved　解決すべき問題

☐ got to work on it　それに取りかかった

☐ this service doesn't come cheap　このサービスは安くはない

☐ Like I said　先ほど申し上げたとおり

TASKの解答例

メモを取るポイント

1. ［質問訳］アライブハウスとは何ですか？

   The name of the speaker's interior-plant design service.（話し手の会社が提供する室内植物デザインサービスの名称）

2. ［質問訳］その会社は何を扱っていますか？

   Living plants (to make rooms and houses greener).（［部屋や家の緑化を進めるための］生きている植物）

3. ［質問訳］その会社は家庭に何を取り込みますか？

   Nature.（自然）

4. ［質問訳］設置終了時には何が見られますか？

   Beautiful plants (that are now a living part of your house).（［家の中の生命力あふれる部分になった］美しい植物）

5. ［質問訳］この会社のオーナーはなぜこの事業を始めたのですか？

   Because he was terrible with houseplants.（観葉植物［の世話］が大の苦手だったから）

6. ［質問訳］この会社のオーナーは何の訓練を受けましたか？

   An engineer.（エンジニア）

7. ［質問訳］彼が開発した鉢植えはどんなものに見えましたか？

   They had terrifying science-fiction machines attached to them.（SFに出てくるようなゾッとする機械が取り付けられていた）

8. ［質問訳］その会社のオーナーの妻は何を学んでいましたか？

   Interior design.（インテリアデザイン）

9. ［質問訳］その会社のオーナーとその妻はどのようにして共同作業をしたのですか？

   They put their ideas together.（二人のアイデアを組み合わせた）

10. ［質問訳］その会社のオーナーは価格について何と言っていますか？

    It doesn't come cheap.（安くはあがらない）

追加の質問と応答例

• Your prices are much higher than those of other gardeners. Is it possible to get a discount?（他の造園業者と比べて料金がかなり高いのですね。割引は可能ですか）

  — Not really. Our services are worth the price.（難しいですね。当社のサービスには料金なりの価値がありますので）

  — It depends. If a similar service is offered at a lower price, ask our sales rep.（時と場合によりけりです。同様のサービスがより低価格で提供されていれば、当社販売担当者にお尋ねください）

- What is the biggest difference between your service and your competitors'?（御社のサービスと競合他社のサービスとの最大の違いは何ですか）
  — I don't think we have competitors because our service is unique.（当社のサービスは唯一無二のものなので、競合相手はいないと考えています）
  — Our sophisticated designs, the selection of plants we use and the speed in which we do it all — I can't pick just one difference.（当社の洗練されたデザイン、使用する植物の選定、これらすべてを行うスピード——ひとつだけ選ぶことはできません）
- How are your services evaluated?（御社のサービスの評価はどうですか）
  — The customer feedback is all on our website. We're No. 1 in the area.（お客様からのご意見はすべて当社のサイトに掲載されています。地域で一番です）
  — Here are the results of the customer survey. Nearly 80 percent of the respondents say they are highly satisfied.（こちらが顧客アンケートの結果です。ほぼ8割の回答者が非常に満足しているとおっしゃっています）

誰かにインタビューするつもりで、想定問答を考えよう！

聞き取りのコツ

自社の業務内容が他社より優れていることを述べるときの表現を聞き取り、自分でも使えるようにしましょう。

● **定型表現だけにとらわれない**

you're not just choosing … の not just を聞いて、not only/just A but also B の表現ではないかと考えたり、but also a way that is tidy and considered と聞いて、not only を聞き逃したのではないかと焦ったりするなら、定型表現にとらわれ過ぎのサインです。

　前者は、「単に…を選んでいるだけではありません」と but also がなくても完結しており、後者は直前の in a comprehensive way に対して付け加えている言い方です。定番中の定番である not only/just A but also B は重宝する言い方ですが、100%その形で使われるわけではありません。頭をやわらかくして聞くように心がけましょう。

● **説明の前に注意を引く**

自社の業務内容を説明する前に、That's almost the opposite of what we're trying to do. とインタビュアーの挙げた例を強く否定しています。単なる No. や Not really. ではなく、almost the opposite（ほぼ正反対）という表現で、聞き手の注意を引いています。

● **強調する**

他社、または他者より優れていることを表すには、やはり比較級がよく使われます。ただ、いつもいつも単に better than … とするよりは、ときには the results, I think, are far better than … のように、far をつけて強調したほうが効果的。far 以外に even、much、a lot にも、比較級を強める用法があります。

Unit
5

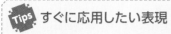

Break that down for me a little bit.
→ break down は「(機械などを) 分解する」以外に、「(話の内容を) 詳細に述べる」の意味でも使われます。また、a little bit (ほんの少しだけ) と言ってはいますが、これは頼みごとをする際の常套句のようなもので、実際にはしっかりと話を掘り下げています。

I was terrible with houseplants.
→「…が苦手だ」は be poor at ... または be not good at ... で表せますが、ここでは terrible を使って「…が大の苦手だ」とやや誇張して言っています。

We're meant to live this way.
→ be meant to ... は「本来…することになっている」の意味。It was meant to be a joke, but she took it seriously. (冗談のつもりだったけど、彼女は本気にした) などのように、人だけでなく物に対してもよく使われます。

74

4 では英文を見ながら、もう一度、聞きましょう。

10

Interviewer: Tell me a little about AliveHouse and what you do.

Lau: So, AliveHouse is the name for our interior plant design service. We are basically interior designers working with living plants to make rooms and homes greener in the easiest way possible for owners. So our core beliefs are ease-of-use and full living-space integration.

Interviewer: Break that down for me a little bit. I mean, clearly you're not just choosing some potted plants to sprinkle around the client's home.

Lau: No. That's almost the opposite of what we're trying to do. OK, let me start with "full living-space integration." We believe that we can really bring nature into a home in a comprehensive way but also in a way that is tidy and considered. So, when we take on a job, it really is a renovation. The greenery will be built into the walls or floor, or suspended from the ceiling, along with the systems that will keep it watered and give it light. There are many, many different ways that we do this, but basically, at the end of the installation, the only things you see are the beautiful plants that are now a living part of your house.

Interviewer: And what about the ease-of-use?

Lau: Well, I started this because I was terrible with houseplants. Just terrible. I just couldn't keep them alive! And the more I read about the subject, the more I realized that every plant, every species, has different needs. Now, I was trained as an engineer, so to me, this seemed like a problem to be solved. I thought, "What could I build that could automate this?" So I got to work on it, and, much to my wife's horror, I ended up with potted plants that had these terrifying science-fiction machines attached to them. Meanwhile, my wife was

Unit
5

learning interior design, and we just kind of put the two ideas together and hid the mechanics.

Interviewer: So, are you a bigger fan of houseplants now?

Lau: Oh, absolutely. I mean, the more I worked on this, the more I started to see how they just lift a person's mood. I honestly believe we're meant to live this way, surrounded by nature. It actually makes us healthier. People who can't imagine caring for plants are entirely missing out on this ... this primal feeling of belonging.

Interviewer: I imagine this service doesn't come cheap.

Lau: Well, unfortunately, it does not! Ha-ha. Like I said, it is a kind of minor renovation. The systems we install require a lot of fine-tuning. So, yes. You need to think of it as interior design. But the results, I think, are far better than, you know, a little potted palm tree in the corner.

日本語訳

インタビュアー：アライブハウスと御社の業務について少し教えてください。

ラウ：アライブハウスは当社の室内植物デザインサービスの名前です。私たちは基本的にインテリアデザイナーであり、家主様にとってできる限り簡単な方法でお部屋やお住まいの緑化を進めるために、生きた植物を取り扱っている会社です。ですから、当社の基本信念は使いやすさと生活空間の全体的な統合です。

インタビュアー：それをもう少し細かく説明してください。つまり、御社がなさっているのは、単にお客様の家の周りに点在させる鉢植えを選ぶのは、明らかに違いますよね。

ラウ：違いますね。それは私たちがやろうとしているのとは、ほぼ正反対のことです。「生活空間の全体的な統合」からご説明を始めましょう。私たちは、自然を住居の中に総合的に取り込むことが実際にできると信じていますが、それだけではなく、その方法は整然として、考慮されたものでもあります。ですから、当社が仕事を引き受けると、実際には改修工事をすることになります。壁や床に緑を植えたり、天井から吊り下げたりし、同時に、たえず水やりをしたり、光を当てたりするシステムを設置します。これには実にたくさんの方法がありますが、基本的には設置後に目にするのは家の中の生命力あふれる部分になった美しい植物だけです。

インタビュアー：使いやすさについてはいかがですか？

ラウ：私がこの事業を始めたのは、私自身が観葉植物の世話が大の苦手だったからです。本当にひどかったんです。生かしておくことができませんでした！　このテーマについて学べば学ぶほど、植物や種ごとに必要とすることが異なると気づきました。つまり、エンジニアとしての訓練を受けていたので、私にとってこれは解決すべき問題のように思えたのです。「自動化を可能にするには、どんな装置をつくればいいだろうか？」と考えました。そして、その作業に取りかかることになったのですが、妻を恐怖に陥れたことに、私は最終的に SF に出てくるゾッとするような機械を鉢植えに取り付けていたのです。一方、妻はインテリアデザインを学んでいましたので、私たちは双方の

アイデアを組み合わせて、その機械装置を外からは見えなくしました。

インタビュアー：そうして今では、観葉植物が以前より好きになったのですか？

ラウ：もちろんです。つまり、これに取り組めば取り組むほど、植物がいかに人の気分を高揚させるかがわかってきました。私たちはこのように自然に囲まれて生きる存在なのだと心から信じています。そうすることが私たちをより健康にしてくれます。植物を愛でることを想像できない人たちは、この…この原始的な帰属感を完全に逃してしまっています。

インタビュアー：こうしたサービスは安くはないのではないでしょうね。

ラウ：残念ながら安くはありません！　はは。ええ。先ほども申し上げたとおり、ちょっとした修繕工事です。私たちが設置するシステムは、多くの微調整を必要とします。ええ。インテリアデザインとしてお考えいただく必要があります。しかし、その結果は部屋の隅に置かれたかわいらしい鉢植えのヤシの木よりもはるかに良いものになる、と私は思います。

Unit
5

5 ダイアログの内容について下記の設問に答えましょう。解答と解説、翻訳はページの下にあります。

Q1 What does the man's company do?
- (A) They put plants around the clients' houses.
- (B) They make rooms and homes greener.
- (C) They water and give light to plants.
- (D) They renovate office buildings.

Q2 How does the man believe people should live?
- (A) Belonging to a society.
- (B) Putting ideas together.
- (C) Surrounded by nature.
- (D) Trained as professionals.

解答と解説

Q1 解答 (B)
男性の会社はどのような業務を行なっていますか?
(A) 顧客の家の周りに植物を配置している。
(B) 部屋や家の緑化を進めている。
(C) 植物に水をやったり、光を当てたりしている。
(D) 事務所用ビルの改装を行なっている。

解説 男性が最初に業務概要を、We are basically interior designers working with living plants to make rooms and homes greener ... と説明しているので、正解は (B) です。

Q2 解答 (C)
人はどのようにして生きるべきだと男性は考えていますか?
(A) 社会に帰属しながら。
(B) アイデアを組み合わせながら。
(C) 自然に囲まれて。
(D) 専門家として訓練を受けて。

解説 以前よりも観葉植物が好きになったかと聞かれた男性が、I honestly believe we're meant to live this way, surrounded by nature. と言っています。設問の should はこの be meant to を言い換えたもの。したがって、正解は (C) です。

6 最後に、スラッシュの箇所でリピートしてみます。かたまりごとに、意味が
わかっているか確認しながら口に出してみましょう。

🎧 11

Interviewer: Tell me a little about AliveHouse / and what you do. //

Lau: So, AliveHouse is the name for our interior plant design service. // We are basically interior designers working with living plants / to make rooms and homes greener / in the easiest way possible for owners. // So our core beliefs are ease-of-use / and full living-space integration. //

Interviewer: Break that down for me a little bit. // I mean, / clearly you're not just choosing some potted plants / to sprinkle around the client's home. //

Unit
5

Lau: No. // That's almost the opposite of what we're trying to do. // OK, let me start with "full living-space integration." // We believe that / we can really bring nature into a home in a comprehensive way / but also in a way that is tidy and considered. // So, when we take on a job, / it really is a renovation. // The greenery will be built into the walls or floor, / or suspended from the ceiling, / along with the systems / that will keep it watered and give it light. // There are many, many different ways that we do this, / but basically, at the end of the installation, / the only things you see are the beautiful plants / that are now a living part of your house. //

Interviewer: And what about the ease-of-use? //

Lau: Well, I started this / because I was terrible with houseplants. // Just terrible. // I just couldn't keep them alive! // And the more I read about the subject, / the more I realized that every plant, every species, / has different needs. // Now, I was trained as an engineer, /

so to me, / this seemed like a problem to be solved. // I thought, / "What could I build that could automate this?" // So I got to work on it, / and, much to my wife's horror, / I ended up with potted plants / that had these terrifying science-fiction machines attached to them. // Meanwhile, my wife was learning interior design, / and we just kind of put the two ideas together / and hid the mechanics. //

Interviewer: So, are you a bigger fan of houseplants now? //

Lau: Oh, absolutely. // I mean, the more I worked on this, / the more I started to see / how they just lift a person's mood. // I honestly believe we're meant to live this way, / surrounded by nature. // It actually makes us healthier. // People who can't imagine caring for plants / are entirely missing out on this / ... this primal feeling of belonging. //

Interviewer: I imagine this service doesn't come cheap. //

Lau: Well, unfortunately, it does not! // Ha-ha. // Like I said, / it is a kind of minor renovation. // The systems we install / require a lot of fine-tuning. // So, yes. // You need to think of it as interior design. // But the results, / I think, are far better than, you know, / a little potted palm tree in the corner. //

Unit
5

green thumb（緑の親指）とは、
「園芸の才能」を意味します。

Listening を鍛える！

Chapter 2
聞いた情報を相手に伝える　上級編

ここでは、以下のようなモノローグ（一人の話者による語り）を聞きます。トピックも専門的なものが増えますが、興味のあるものから聞いてみるといいでしょう。耳だけでは理解できない場合には、単語の意味もしっかり押さえてトライしてみましょう。

Unit 6　完全に平等な社会を目指し
〈社会問題／ニュース〉

Unit 7　あらがえぬ魅力を伝える
〈商品の紹介／ラジオ CM〉

Unit 8　それはゴミではありません
〈リサイクル／ドキュメンタリー〉

Unit 9　目は口ほどに…
〈心理学／レクチャー〉

Unit 10　発展めざましい医学界
〈医学／ニュース特集〉

🎧 12-14   **LISTENING**

難易度 ●●●● 4 | 290語（短い） | 社会問題／ニュース | ▩ 男

TASK

1 ニュースを聞いて、その内容を把握します。特に、ニュースで特徴的な「リード段落」の役割を理解し、自分でも書いてみることで、ニュース英語により深く慣れていきましょう。   [**学習目標時間20分**]

● 音声を聞いて、下記リード部分の空欄を埋め、その後、与えられた情報をもとに別の記事のリード部分を作ってみましょう。音声は何度聞いてもかまいません。必要に応じて次ページの「単語のヘルプ」も参考にしましょう（解答例はp. 87）。

🎧 12 ┈┈ ◆

A. Fill in the blanks.

LOS ANGELES / SAN FRANCISCO—(1   ) of the LGBT+ community (2   ) to the (3   ) over the weekend in a series of public events (4   ) to support Pride and (5   ) progress in (6   ) and human (7   ). But many of those (8   ) in and (9   ) the protests and (10   ) called (11   ) to the problems of (12   ) and (13   ) they say is often (14   ) in the LGBT+ community.

B. Write a lead paragraph for a news article.

概要：　　　　Acme Industry の主力工場（2003年、長野県で創立）が
　　　　　　　20周年を迎える
工場：　　　　広さ　100エーカー
利点：　　　　1万人を超す雇用／近隣商店の活性化
開設時の懸念：環境への影響
結果：　　　　大気汚染、騒音とも解決

```
_____
_____
_____
_____
```

（ 単語のヘルプ ）

- [ ] LGBT+　レズビアン、ゲイ、バイセクシュアル、トランスジェンダーなどの性的少数派
- [ ] take to the streets　デモ行進をする
- [ ] Pride　＊あとに出てくる Pride & Freedom（性的少数派の団体）を短く言ったもの
- [ ] participate in 〜　〜に参加する
- [ ] observe　見物する
- [ ] rally　集会
- [ ] call attention to 〜　〜に注意を促す
- [ ] racism　人種差別
- [ ] discrimination　不公平な扱い、差別
- [ ] inflatable　空気注入式の、膨らませることができる
- [ ] hybrid　混合の
- [ ] meet-up　会合
- [ ] legalization　合法化
- [ ] outspoken　（意見などが）率直な
- [ ] persistent　いつまでも続く
- [ ] be held accountable　責任がある
- [ ] ethnicity　民族性

Unit
6

以下のチャンクを聞き取るよう気を付けながら、もう一度、音声を聞きましょう。聞き取れたら □ にチェックを入れましょう。

🎧 12 ⋯⋯⋯⋯⋯⋯⋯⋯⋯⋯⋯⋯⋯⋯⋯⋯⋯⋯⋯⋯⋯⋯⋯⋯⋯⋯⋯⋯⋯⋯◆

☐ drew a large crowd of marchers 大勢のデモ参加者を呼び込んだ

☐ They were joined by ... 彼らには…が加わった

☐ much work remains to be done すべきことはまだ多い

☐ called attention to the persistent problem なかなか解決しない問題に注意を促した

☐ have experienced repeated discrimination 度重なる差別を受けてきた

☐ should be held accountable 責任を取るべきである

☐ came under criticism 批判を浴びた

TASKの解答例

A. Fill in the blanks.

LOS ANGELES / SAN FRANCISCO —[1](Members) of the LGBT+ community [2](took) to the [3](streets) over the weekend in a series of public events [4](organized) to support Pride and [5](celebrate) progress in [6](civil) and human [7](rights). But many of those [8](participating) in and [9](observing) the protests and [10](rallies) called [11](attention) to the problems of [12](racism) and [13](discrimination) they say is often [14](ignored) in the LGBT+ community.

B. Write a lead paragraph for a news article.

Founded in 2003 in Nagano, Acme Industry has set up production facilities around the country. This year, the main factory celebrates its 20th anniversary along with the partnership companies. The 100-acre plant has contributed to the local economy by creating more than 10,000 jobs and boosting sales of the shops and stores in the neighborhood. Although there once was a concern over damage to the environment, the company's efforts have been successful in reducing the air and noise pollution caused by cars and trucks going in and out of the factory.

Unit
6

日本語訳

2003年に長野県で設立されたアクメ産業は、これまで国内に数々の生産拠点を建設してきました。今年、主力工場が協力会社とともに20周年記念を迎えます。広さ100エーカーを誇るこの工場は、1万人を超える雇用を生み、近隣商店の売上を押し上げることで、地元経済に貢献してきました。かつては環境被害に対する懸念がありましたが、同社の努力によって工場に出入りする車やトラックがもたらす大気汚染や騒音公害を減らすことに成功しました。

答え合わせのあとに、音声でも確認しましょう（A はトラック12参照）。

 13

3 聞き取りのコツ

ニュースの文章構成の特徴を知ることが、正確な聞き取りにつながります。

● ニュースの構成
ニュースではまず大まかな内容 (リード) が述べられ、その後、詳細が続きます。
Members of the LGBT+ community took to the streets ... から、they say is often ignored in the LGBT+ community.までがリード (lead paragraph) の部分です。その内容を具体的に述べているのが、In Los Angeles ... から最後まで。同じようなことが2度聞こえてくるのはそのためです。リードの内容をきちんと把握すれば、全体の理解度が上がります。

● 逆接の接続詞に注意
このニュースは、
Members of the LGBT+ community took to the streets ...と始まっていて、LGBTを差別する世の中の風潮に対して抗議している内容だと思いきや、But many of those ... called attention to the problems ... often ignored in the LGBT+ community.と、LGBT社会の中でも問題があると伝えています。逆接の接続詞のあとには本当に言いたいことが続く場合も多いので、butやhoweverなどは「再度集中せよ」の標識だととらえましょう。

● 無生物主語
英語では、
the March for Pride & Freedom drew a large crowd gathered ...
Similar events ... also combined ...
much work remains to be done ...
のように無生物を主語とする文もよく使われます。このニュースでは人の行動を伝えるものなので、人が主語の文のほうが多いのですが、上の3文を
a large crowd gathered for the March for Pride & Freedom ...
People who attended similar events ... also had ...
they still need to do much work ...
とすると文全体のリズムが単調になってしまうので、あえて無生物主語の文を織り交ぜるという手法が使われます。

すぐに応用したい表現

many of those participating in and observing the protests and rallies called attention to ...

→この those は people の意味。ing 形の動詞を続けて、「…する人たち」を表しています。those who participated in ... などの those who ... に加えて、この those -ing も覚えておきましょう。

these advancements are to be celebrated

→ be to は「予定」「義務」などを表す言い方です。ここでは「こうした進歩は称賛されるべきだ」の意味。日常会話でも He is to leave tomorrow.（彼は明日出発する予定だ）、You are to keep quiet.（静かにしていなさい）のように使います。

LGBT+ businesses should be held accountable just as large corporations increasingly are.

→ just as で「〜も同様に」と付け加える用法です。無駄な繰り返しを避けた省略形（ここでは are held accountable を are だけで表している）を自分でも使えるようにしましょう。

Unit
6

89

4 では英文を見ながら、もう一度、聞きましょう。

🎧 12 ....◆

LOS ANGELES / SAN FRANCISCO—Members of the LGBT+ community took to the streets over the weekend in a series of public events organized to support Pride and celebrate progress in civil and human rights. But many of those participating in and observing the protests and rallies called attention to the problems of racism and discrimination they say is often ignored in the LGBT+ community.

In Los Angeles, the March for Pride & Freedom drew a large crowd of marchers who gathered at Pacific River Park. They were joined by more than 13,000 more online participants, using an inflatable outdoor jumbo screen to create a hybrid online in-person rally and live concert.

Similar events in San Francisco and several other cities also combined online meetings, concerts and talks with outdoor marches and meet-ups in public parks and plazas. Representatives of LGBT+ organizations noted major advancements such as the legalization of same-sex marriage. They said that while these advancements are to be celebrated, much work remains to be done toward achieving full equality throughout society.

But many of the most outspoken of the presentations called attention to the persistent problem of racial discrimination within the LGBT+ community. Several speakers called attention to a recent study by the Goodsen Equity Project, noting that a large majority of Black, Asian and other minority LGBT+ people have experienced repeated discrimination from members of the community.

Micah Graven, an organizer of the San Francisco event, said that LGBT+ businesses should be held accountable just as large corporations increasingly are. Graven recently made news by encouraging the top three dating sites serving the LGBT+ community to remove "ethnicity filters" from their websites, which came under criticism for enabling users to select prospective partners solely by race.

┌─────────┐
│ 日本語訳 │
└─────────┘

ロサンゼルス／サンフランシスコ発 —— LGBT+ コミュニティのメンバーが週末、『プライド』を支援し、公民権と人権の進歩を祝うために開催された一連の公開イベントにおいてデモを行った。しかし、抗議活動や集会の参加者および見学者の多くは、LGBT+ コミュニティ内でしばしば無視されていると彼らが言っている人種差別や不公平な扱いの問題に注目するよう求めた。

ロサンゼルスでは、『プライド＆フリーダム・マーチ』が開催され、パシフィック・リバー・パークに集まった大勢のデモ参加者を呼び込んだ。さらに1万3000人を超えるオンライン参加者があり、空気注入式屋外ジャンボスクリーンを使って、オンライン・対面混合型の集会とライブコンサートを行った。

サンフランシスコなどいくつかの都市でも同様のイベントが開かれ、そこでもオンラインでの会合、コンサート、講演会が、野外行進や公園や広場での会合と同時に開催された。LGBT+ 団体の代表者らは、同性婚の合法化などの大きな進展に言及した。彼らは、これらの進歩は称賛されるべきだが、社会全体の完全な平等を達成するためには、まだ多くのすべきことが残っていると述べた。

しかし、発表の中で最も率直な意見を述べる人たちの多くは、LGBT+ コミュニティ内の人種差別というなかなか解決しない問題への注意を促していた。何人かの講演者は、グッドセン・エクイティ・プロジェクトによる最近の調査に注目するよう呼びかけ、黒人、アジア人など少数民族のLGBT+ の人々の大多数が、コミュニティのメンバーから度重なる差別を受けていると指摘した。

サンフランシスコ大会の主催者であるミカ・グレーブン氏は、まさに大企業がますますそうなっているように、LGBT+ 企業も責任を取るべきだと述べた。グレーブン氏は最近、LGBT+ コミュニティにサービスを提供しているトップ3の出会い系サイトに対して、パートナー候補者を単に人種で選ぶことを可能にするとして批判を浴びた「民族フィルター」をサイトから削除するよう促したとして、ニュースに取り上げられていた。

Unit
6

ニュースの内容について下記の設問に答えましょう。解答と解説、翻訳は
ページの下にあります。

Q1 Why did those people take to the streets?
  (A) To host the protests and rallies
  (B) To ignore racism and discrimination
  (C) To create online concerts
  (D) To celebrate progress in civil and human rights

Q2 According to a study, who have minority LGBT+ people received
discrimination from?
  (A) Black and Asian people
  (B) Memebers of their community
  (C) The organizer of the event
  (D) Speakers at the rallies

解答と解説

Q1 解答（D）
その人々はなぜデモ行進をしたのですか?
(A) 反対運動と集会を主催するため
(B) 人種差別と不公平な扱いを無視するため
(C) オンラインでのコンサートを作り上げるため
(D) 市民権と人権における進歩を祝うため

解説 デモに参加した目的については、to support Pride and celebrate progress in
civil and human rightsと述べられています。このcelebrate以下である (D) が正解です。

Q2 解答（B）
ある研究によれば、少数派民族のLGBT+の人たちは誰から差別を受けていますか?
(A) 黒人とアジア人
(B) 自分たちのコミュニティの人たち
(C) このイベントの主催者
(D) 集会での演説者

解説 少数派民族のLGBT+の人たちについては、a large majority of Black, Asian
and other minority LGBT+ people have experienced repeated discrimination
from members of the communityとLGBT+の人たちから度重なる差別を受けていると
述べられているので、正解は (B) です。

最後に、スラッシュの箇所でリピートしてみます。かたまりごとに、意味がわかっているか確認しながら口に出してみましょう。

 14

LOS ANGELES / SAN FRANCISCO — / Members of the LGBT+ community / took to the streets over the weekend / in a series of public events / organized to support Pride / and celebrate progress in civil and human rights. // But many of those participating in / and observing the protests and rallies / called attention to the problems of racism and discrimination / they say is often ignored in the LGBT+ community. //

In Los Angeles, / the March for Pride & Freedom / drew a large crowd of marchers / who gathered at Pacific River Park. // They were joined by more than 13,000 more online participants, / using an inflatable outdoor jumbo screen / to create a hybrid online in-person rally and live concert. //

Similar events in San Francisco and several other cities / also combined online meetings, concerts and talks / with outdoor marches and meet-ups in public parks and plazas. // Representatives of LGBT+ organizations noted / major advancements such as the legalization of same-sex marriage. // They said that while these advancements are to be celebrated, / much work remains to be done / toward achieving full equality throughout society. //

But many of the most outspoken of the presentations / called attention to the persistent problem of racial discrimination / within the LGBT+ community. // Several speakers called attention to a recent study / by the Goodsen Equity Project, / noting that a large majority of Black, Asian and other minority LGBT+ people / have experienced repeated discrimination from members of the community. //

Unit
6

Micah Graven, an organizer of the San Francisco event, said that / LGBT+ businesses should be held accountable / just as large corporations increasingly are. // Graven recently made news by encouraging the top three dating sites serving the LGBT+ community / to remove "ethnicity filters" from their websites, / which came under criticism for enabling users / to select prospective partners solely by race. //

Unit
6

LGBTQ という言い方もあります。
Q は questioning、
「性別を決めていない人」を
指すことが多いです。

Unit 7　あらがえぬ魅力を伝える

LISTENING

難易度 ●●○○○ 2　　約200語（短い）　　商品の紹介／ラジオCM　　🇺🇸 女

TASK

1　ラジオCMを聞いたあなたが、その商品を買おうと思ったきっかけは何だったのでしょうか。　　[**学習目標時間20分**]

●音声を聞いて、①広告独特の比喩表現（英語）とそれらが与える印象（日本語）をメモし、その後、②商品購入を決めた理由（として考えられること）をいくつか述べてみましょう。必要に応じて次ページの「単語のヘルプ」も参考にしましょう（解答例はp. 99）。

🎧 **15**

① 広告独特の比喩表現とその与える印象

例：
like silk against your skin → 口当たりが滑らかな

---

② 購入を決めた理由

I have decided to buy this product because ...

-
-
-
-
-

(単語のヘルプ)

- [ ] candlelit　ろうそくが灯った
- [ ] sensation　大評判のもの
- [ ] fashion　作る
- [ ] hand down　後世に伝える（受動態で使われることが多い）
- [ ] chocolatier　チョコレート職人
- [ ] ingredient　原料
- [ ] vibrant　鮮やかな
- [ ] glossy　光沢のある
- [ ] buzz　ざわめく、うなる
- [ ] indulgent　気ままにさせる、寛大な
- [ ] wickedly　最高に
- [ ] line　取扱商品

Unit
7

🎧 15 ‥‥‥◆

☐ has been handed down through generations　何世代にも渡って受け継がれてきた

☐ Using all-natural ingredients　完全天然材料を使って

☐ you deserve the best　あなたは最高のものを受け取るにふさわしい

☐ filled with all the flavors you desire　あなたが望むすべての味が詰まった

☐ as the weather cools down　天候が涼しくなるにつれて

☐ see our latest lines　当社の最新取扱商品を見る

TASK の解答例

A. 広告独特の比喩表現とその与える印象

like silk against your skin →口当たりが滑らかな

the warmth of a candlelit room →温かみのある

the moon on a summer night →ロマンティックな

the black velvet of an evening dress →優雅な

Europe's best chocolate makers →信頼できる

the carefully guarded Chimay recipe →他にはない

been handed down through generations →伝統がある

a glossy dark-chocolate coating →食欲をそそる

undeniably luxurious →絶対的においしい

a gift that won't soon be forgotten →記憶に残る

have your guests buzzing →人を喜ばせる

wickedly rich →甘美な

B. 購入を決めた理由

I have decided to buy this product because...

・it sounds sophisticated.（洗練された響きがある）

・it has attracted so many people.（これまで数多くの人たちを魅了してきた）

・it is luxurious.（高級感がある）

・it should be incredibly delicious.（驚くほどおいしいはずだ）

・it is something you should have at least once in your life.（一生に一度は口に
すべきものだ）

Unit
7

3 聞き取りのコツ

広告 (コマーシャル) は雰囲気で伝える部分もあるため、特に出だしを理解するには想像力が必要となります。また、人じさな表現も多く、やや戸惑うこともあるかもしれませんが、聞き進めていけば必ず商品名などが出てきて、そこで点と点がつながり全体像が見えてきます。

● 注意を引く導入部分

いきなり、Our chocolate is the best in the world. などと始めるのではなく、導入部分で聞いている人たちに「何の話だろう?」と思わせる attention getter を使うのが広告の常套手段です。ここでは、

It's a feeling — like silk against your skin, or the warmth of a candlelit room. It's the moon on a summer night, or the black velvet of an evening dress.

までは、まるで衣料品か寝具の話のようです。しかし、

It's a sensation. It's a tradition.

で「おや?」と思わせ、最後に、

It's Chimay Chocolate.

とチョコレートの宣伝であることを明らかにしています。

● 大げさな言い回し

目立つことが大事な広告にとっては、非日常的な表現を使うのは当然のことです。たとえば、

you deserve the best (あなたは最高のものを持つに値する)

a truly indulgent, wickedly rich treat (真に人を甘やかし、邪悪なほどに濃厚なごちそう)

のような言い方は普段の会話では使われません。こうした部分を、頭の中で直訳しながら聞いていると話の全体が見えなくなってしまいます。「要は何が言いたいのか」をとらえるようにしましょう。

● 最後の一押し

商品説明ののち、最後に

What are you waiting for? (もう何を待つこともないでしょう)

に続き、畳みかけるように購買行動の開始を促しています。商品名を繰り返すことも忘れていません。広告の内容を知るだけが目的であれば、ここはあまり聞く必要もありませんが、営業活動などで締めの一言を決めたい方は、この話のテンポはかなり参考になるでしょう。

すぐに応用したい表現

It's a sensation.
→ sensation（大評判）は数えられないはずなのになぜ a が付いているんだろうと思った方もいるかもしれません。この sensation は「大評判を引き起こすもの」「世間を騒がせるもの」という可算名詞として使われています。He has been a major influence in my life.（彼は私の人生に多大な影響を与えた人物です）の influence 同様、可算名詞と不可算名詞の両方の用法を持つ名詞です。

the carefully guarded Chimay recipe has been handed down through generations ...
→ be handed down（継承される）には from generation to generation や over the generations といった言い方も続きます。伝統ある事物について説明する際に欠かせない表現です。

What are you waiting for?
→ここでは「この商品の良さはもうおわかりでしょうから、すぐにお買い求めください」といった気持ちで使われていますが、日常生活では「何を待っているのですか」だけでなく、「何をグズグズしてるの、早くしなさい」と相手を急かすときにもよく使われます。

Unit
7

4 では英文を見ながら、もう一度、聞きましょう。

🎧 **15** ....◆

It's a feeling — like silk against your skin, or the warmth of a candlelit room. It's the moon on a summer night, or the black velvet of an evening dress. It's a sensation. It's a tradition. It's Chimay Chocolate.

Fashioned with old-world care by Europe's best chocolate makers, the carefully guarded Chimay recipe has been handed down through generations of chocolatiers. Using all-natural ingredients, we have crafted the finest chocolates in the world because you deserve the best.

Try our classic variety box — vibrant fruit or nut centers, wrapped in a glossy dark-chocolate coating. Or order a selection box of chocolate truffles — rich and creamy, undeniably luxurious, filled with all the flavors you desire. It's a gift that won't soon be forgotten. Or enjoy a box of mint thins — a perfectly elegant after-dinner choice that will have your guests buzzing.

And as the weather cools down, enjoy Chimay's newest addition — our Chateau Hot Chocolate — in milk-chocolate, dark-chocolate, white-chocolate and chocolate-orange flavors. Just mix with hot milk for a truly indulgent, wickedly rich treat.

What are you waiting for? Indulge yourself and your family. Search for Chimay Chocolate to find your nearest boutique today and see our latest lines. Chimay Chocolate — taste the tradition.

> **日本語訳**

この感覚は、まるでシルクの肌触り、もしくは、キャンドルに照らされた部屋の暖かさ。夏の夜の月、またはイブニングドレスの黒いビロード。センセーションを起こすもの。伝統的なもの。それは、チメイ・チョコレートです。

　ヨーロッパの一流チョコレートメーカーが昔ながらのこだわりをもって作り上げたチメイのレシピは厳重に門外不出で、何世代にもわたってチョコレート職人に受け継がれてきました。私たちは完全天然素材を使用し、世界最高級のチョコレートを完成させましたが、それはお客様が最上のものをお受け取りになるのにふさわしい方だからです。

　鮮やかなフルーツやナッツの中心部を光沢のあるダークチョコレートでコーティングした、定番のバ

ラエティボックスをお試しください。または、チョコレートトリュフのセレクションボックスをご注文ください──そこには、濃厚かつクリーミーで、紛れもなく贅沢で、あなたが望むすべての味が詰まっています。それはすぐには忘れることのない贈り物です。または、お客様をざわめかせる完璧にエレガントな夕食後の逸品、箱入りミントシンズをお楽しみください。

　そして、天候が涼しくなったら、ミルクチョコレート、ダークチョコレート、ホワイトチョコレート、チョコレートオレンジのフレーバーがある、チメイの最新作シャトーホットチョコレートをお楽しみください。ホットミルクと混ぜるだけで、まさにすべてを包み込み、最高に濃厚な甘味になります。

　もうためらうことはありませんね？　ご自分とご家族を喜ばせましょう。チメイ・チョコレートを検索して最寄りの専門店を探し、最新のラインナップをご覧ください。チメイ・チョコレート──伝統を味わうチョコレートです。

Unit
7

5 コマーシャルの内容について下記の設問に答えましょう。解答と解説、翻訳はページの下にあります。

Q1 Which of the following best describes the chocolate?
(A) Warm
(B) Glossy
(C) New
(D) Traditional

Q2 What do they suggest we do when the weather cools down?
(A) Enjoy hot chocolate
(B) Indulge our family
(C) Buy mint thins
(D) Find one of their shops

解答と解説

Q1 解答（D）
次のうち、このチョコレートを最も的確に描写しているのはどれですか？
(A) 暖かい
(B) 光沢のある
(C) 新しい
(D) 伝統的な

解説 最初にIt's a tradition.と、次にrecipe has been handed down through generationsと、そして、最後にtast the tradition.とその伝統を売りにしているので、正解は(D)です。

Q2 解答（A）
寒くなったらどうするように提案していますか？
(A) ホットチョコレートを楽しむ
(B) 家族を甘やかす
(C) ミントシンズを買う
(D) 同社の店舗を見つける

解説 as the weather cools downの直後のenjoy Chimay's newest additionからは何のことかはっきりしませんが、additionの説明としてour Chateau Hot Chocolateと続いているので、(A)が正解だとわかります。

最後に、スラッシュの箇所でリピートしてみます。かたまりごとに、意味が
わかっているか確認しながら口に出してみましょう。

 16

It's a feeling / — like silk against your skin, / or the warmth of a candlelit room. // It's the moon on a summer night, / or the black velvet of an evening dress. // It's a sensation. // It's a tradition. // It's Chimay Chocolate. //

Fashioned with old-world care by Europe's best chocolate makers, / the carefully guarded Chimay recipe / has been handed down through generations of chocolatiers. // Using all-natural ingredients, / we have crafted the finest chocolates in the world / because you deserve the best. //

Try our classic variety box / — vibrant fruit or nut centers, / wrapped in a glossy dark-chocolate coating. // Or order a selection box of chocolate truffles / — rich and creamy, undeniably luxurious, / filled with all the flavors you desire. // It's a gift that won't soon be forgotten. // Or enjoy a box of mint thins / — a perfectly elegant after-dinner choice / that will have your guests buzzing. //

And as the weather cools down, / enjoy Chimay's newest addition / — our Chateau Hot Chocolate / — in milk-chocolate, dark-chocolate, white-chocolate and chocolate-orange flavors. // Just mix with hot milk / for a truly indulgent, wickedly rich treat. //

What are you waiting for? // Indulge yourself and your family. // Search for Chimay Chocolate to find your nearest boutique today / and see our latest lines. // Chimay Chocolate / — taste the tradition. //

Unit
7

🎧 17-18   **LISTENING**

| 難易度 ●●●●○ 4 | 約470語（やや長い） | リサイクル／ドキュメンタリー | 男 |

TASK

1 あなたはドキュメンタリーを聞いています。番組後に内容について自分なりの考えをまとめてみましょう。　　　　　[**学習目標時間20分**]

●まず、音声を通して聞きながら、下線部の内容を記号や省略形などを使ってメモしていってください。全体を聞き終えたところで、メモを完全な英文に戻してみます。そのあと、提案内容に賛成する理由と反対する理由の両方を少なくとも3つずつ考えましょう。必要に応じて次ページの「単語のヘルプ」も参考にしましょう（解答例は pp. 109-110）。

🎧 17 ···◆

Paragraph 1
Nationwide, there are billions of 1._____ lying forgotten
in 2._____.

Paragraph 2
They contain thousands of tons of 3._____.

Paragraph 3
As our phones and computers go out of date ever more quickly,
recycling advocates say we should start 4._____.

Paragraph 4
Mining is one of 5._____.

Paragraph 5
As valuable ores become harder to find, 6._____.

Paragraph 6
What you shouldn't do is 7._____.

賛成するとしたらその理由
I'm for this idea because ...

    1. _____
    2. _____
    3. _____

反対するとしたらその理由
I'm against this idea because ...

    1. _____
    2. _____
    3. _____

(単語のヘルプ)

☐ gold mine　金鉱
☐ be tempted to ～　～したい衝動に駆られる
☐ untapped　未利用の、未開発の
☐ gadget　小型機器（スマホなど）
☐ attic　屋根裏部屋
☐ expertise　専門知識
☐ extract　抽出する
☐ ore　鉱石
☐ advocate　推進派、提唱者
☐ urban mining　都市鉱山発掘
☐ run-up　準備段階　＊イギリス英語
☐ nifty　すばらしい
☐ mint　鋳造する
☐ carbon emission　炭素排出量
☐ biodiversity　生物多様性
☐ boost　押し上げる
☐ competitive　競争力のある

Unit
8

2 以下のチャンクを聞き取るよう気を付けながら、もう一度、音声を聞きましょう。聞き取れたら □ にチェックを入れましょう。

🎧 **17** ⋯⋯⋯⋯⋯⋯⋯⋯⋯⋯⋯⋯⋯⋯⋯⋯⋯⋯⋯⋯⋯⋯⋯⋯⋯⋯⋯⋯⋯⋯⋯◆

☐ you might be tempted to ...　あなたは…したくなるかもしれない

☐ have a store of untapped mineral resources　未発掘の鉱物資源を有する

☐ it takes some expertise　ある程度の専門知識が必要だ

☐ With the right knowledge and equipment　正しい知識と器具を持っていれば

☐ in the run-up to the Tokyo Olympic Games　東京オリンピックの準備段階で

☐ responsible for about 40 percent of worldwide carbon emissions
　世界の炭素排出量の約40％の原因である

☐ look with greater interest at ...　より大きな関心を持って…を見る

☐ The time may come when ...　…するときが来るかもしれない

TASK の解答例

聞きながらメモを取るには多少の練習と自分なりの工夫が必要です。以下のイタリック体の
ように、頭文字、最初の数文字、一部の子音、記号、また時には日本語を使ってもけっこう
です。大事なのは、ここから正しい英文（→印の右側）を再生することです。

Paragraph 1

Nationwide, there are billions of 1._____ lying forgotten in
2._____.

1. *o/d com, pri, mob, usless appl* → outdated or broken computers, printers,
   mobile phones and numerous other useless gadgets and appliances
2. *clo, att, bsm, gra* → closets, attics, basements and garages

Paragraph 2

They contain thousands of tons of 3._____.

3. *vlu, mt>co, sl, g, チタン* → valuable metals, like copper, silver, gold and
   titanium

Paragraph 3

As our phones and computers go out of date ever more quickly, recycling
advocates say we should start 4._____.

4. *mng, mts, disc, gad, × thr, lf* → mining the mountains of discarded gadgets
   instead of throwing them into landfill

Paragraph 4

Mining is one of 5._____.

5. *envrn, destr, idst* → the most environmentally destructive industries around

Paragraph 5

As valuable ores become harder to find, 6._____.

6. *co, dg, up, inc* → the cost of digging them up will increase

Paragraph 6

What you shouldn't do is 7._____.

7. *thr, el, trsh* → throw anything electronic in the trash

Unit
8

賛成するとしたらその理由

I'm for this idea because ...

1. it's eco-friendly and good for the next geration.（環境に優しく、次世代にとっていいことだ）

2. we can use those metals for a longer period of time.（そうした金属をより長期間利用できる）

3. it makes no sense to just waste those unused valuable metals.（使わなくなった貴金属をただ無駄にするのでは意味がない）

反対するとしたらその理由

I'm against this idea because ...

1. it takes time, and sometimes money, to have those metals extracted, and I don't think it's worth it.（そうした金属を抽出してもらうには時間と費用がかかり、その価値はないと思う）

2. I don't want to discard any device that has pictures of my family or private information in it.（家族の写真や個人情報が入っているどんなデバイスも捨てたくない）

3. future technologies will be able to replace those metals in computers and phones so we don't need to worry about it now.（未来の技術をもってすれば、コンピューターや電話に入っている金属の代替品を作れるだろうから、今、私たちが心配する必要はない）

3 聞き取りのコツ

● 注意を引く導入部分　その2

Unit 7でも取り上げましたが、導入部分では聞いている人たちの注意を引き、続きを聞きたいという気持ちにさせることが大事です。ここではまず、

If ... there was a gold mine in your backyard（あなたの裏庭に金鉱があったとしたら）

で、「おや?」と思わせ、

no one has such luck（そんな運のいい人はいない）

で、「なんだ、やっぱり」という気持ちにさせてから、

But just about every household ... does have ... mineral resources.（しかし、ほとんどの家庭には鉱物資源が実際にある）

と、「都市鉱山発掘」の話題につなげています。

● 頻繁に使われる並列表現

並列表現とは、A and/or B、A, B and/or C、A, B, C and/or Dのように、同じ要素（品詞など）を並べる用法のことです。何度か読み返せるリーディングとちがって、リスニングでは、「どこで始まり」「（それぞれ長さが異なる場合も多いので）どこまでが一つ一つの要素で」「いくつの要素が並べられているか」を一回聞いただけで判断しなければなりません。ここでも、

outdated or broken computers, printers, mobile phones and numerous other useless gadgets and appliances [A, B, C and Dの形／Dが長い]

valuable metals, like copper, silver, gold and titanium [A, B, C and Dの形／すべて単語1語]

6 million old mobile phones and 72,000 tons of other electronic trash [A and Bの形／どちらも句]

をはじめ、多くの並列表現が使われています。

A↗、B↗and C↘などのように、最後の要素以外は上げ調子で読むという基本ルールはあり、聞きながら判断するヒントにはなりますが、実際には例外も多いので、「並列表現はいつでも現れる」と身構えながら聞く必要があります。

Unit **8**

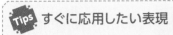 **すぐに応用したい表現**

there are billions of outdated or broken computers ...
→ billions of ... と billion を複数形にして of を続けると「数十億もの…」を意味します。もちろん、thousand、million などについても同様です。また、「数百億もの…」は tens of billions of ...、「数千億もの…」は hundreds of billions of ... と言います。数が多いことを表すときに使える言い方です。

we should start mining the mountains of discarded gadgets instead of throwing them into landfill
→「instead of ... =…の代わりに」と条件反射のように頭に思い浮かぶかもしれませんが、「…ではなく」ととらえたほうがしっくりくる場合があります。ここでは「捨てる代わりに」よりも「捨てるのではなく」のほうがわかりやすいですね。前の文の内容に対して文頭で使われる Instead, ...（そうではなく…だ）も同様です。

why not just keep digging metal up out of the ground?
→ Why not...?（…してはどうでしょうか）の省略された主語が we なのか you なのかは状況によります。いずれにしても、まず Why not と一気に言ってから、述語を続ければいいだけなので、とても使いやすい表現です。

It has tripled over the past 50 years.
→ double（2倍にする）と triple（3倍にする）はよく耳にしますが、quadruple（4倍にする）以降は書かれた文で使われるのが大半です。また、こうした動詞は、Sales have doubled since she joined the company.（彼女が入社してから売り上げが倍になった）、The engineer has doubled the speed of the computer.（その技師がコンピューターの速度を倍にした）のように、自動詞と他動詞両方でよく使われます。

では英文を見ながら、もう一度、聞きましょう。

 17 ....◆

If someone told you there was a gold mine in your backyard, you might be tempted to pick up a shovel and start digging. Virtually no one has such luck, of course. But just about every household in the industrial world does have a store of untapped mineral resources. Nationwide, there are billions of outdated or broken computers, printers, mobile phones and numerous other useless gadgets and appliances lying forgotten in closets, attics, basements and garages.

They contain thousands of tons of valuable metals, like copper, silver, gold and titanium. Of course, it takes some expertise to extract that value. The ordinary consumer might be able to locate and strip the copper wire out of a disused electric motor, but it takes a pro to find gold in an old computer. With the right knowledge and equipment, however, a recycler can extract more gold from a ton of electronic junk than miners get from a ton of high-grade ore.

As our phones and computers go out of date ever more quickly, recycling advocates say we should start mining the mountains of discarded gadgets instead of throwing them into landfill. It's called "urban mining," and it works. One demonstration of this was carried out in Japan in the run-up to the Tokyo Olympic Games. In a very nifty experimental program, consumers from all over Japan donated about 6 million old mobile phones and 72,000 tons of other electronic trash. Recyclers mined it, producing enough metal to mint about 5,000 gold, silver and bronze Olympic medals for the Tokyo Games to be held in 2021.

But why not just keep digging metal up out of the ground? After all, it's always worked before. That's true, but the problem is sustainability. Mining is one of the most environmentally destructive industries around. Natural-resource-extraction industries like gold, copper and silver mining are responsible for about 40 percent of worldwide carbon

Unit
8

emissions and for about 10 percent of biodiversity loss, according to the United Nations. And the rate of extraction is not stable. It has tripled over the past 50 years.

As valuable ores become harder to find, the cost of digging them up will increase. That has already begun to boost the profitability of recycling services. Recyclers are now beginning to look with greater interest at the roughly 50 million tons of electronic waste produced worldwide each year. Many used computer shops will now happily recycle your old computer free of charge.

But in the near future, expect to see much more accommodating services from an increasingly competitive and innovative recycling industry. The time may come when you can exchange your old computers and broken kitchen blenders for good money. For now, the best advice is to recycle immediately, or hold and watch for new developments. What you shouldn't do is throw anything electronic in the trash.

┌─────────────┐
│ **日本語訳** │
└─────────────┘

誰かにあなたの家の裏庭には金鉱があると言われたら、シャベルを手に取って掘り始めてみたくなるかもしれません。もちろん、そのような幸運に恵まれる人はほとんどいません。しかし、工業化社会のほぼ全家庭には未発掘の鉱物資源があります。全国的に見れば、何十億台もの古くなったりこわれたりしたコンピューター、プリンター、携帯電話など数多くの不要な小型機器や電化製品が、クローゼット、屋根裏、地下室、ガレージに眠っています。

そこには銅、銀、金、チタンなどの貴重な金属が何千トンも含まれています。もちろん、そうした貴重なものを抽出するにはある程度の専門知識が必要です。普通の消費者は、使われなくなった電気モーターから銅線を見つけて剥がすことはできるかもしれませんが、古いコンピューターの中から金を見つけるにはプロの力が必要です。しかし、正しい知識と器具があれば、リサイクル業者は、鉱山労働者が大量の高品位鉱石から取り出すよりも多くの金を、電子機器のガラクタの山から取り出すことができます。

私たちの携帯電話やコンピューターがこれまでより急速に時代遅れになる中、リサイクル推進派は、山ほどある捨てられた小型機器をごみ埋立地に廃棄するのではなく、掘り起こし始めるべきだと言います。これは「都市鉱山発掘」と呼ばれ、実効性がある活動です。東京オリンピックの準備段階において、日本でひとつの実証実験が行なわれました。この非常にすばらしい実験企画では、全国の消費者が、約600万台の中古携帯電話と7万2000トンのそれ以外の電子機器廃棄物を寄付しました。リサイクル業者がその採掘を行い、2021年に開催される予定の東京大会用に金メダル、銀メダル、銅メダル約5000個を鋳造するのに十分な量の金属を産出しました。

しかし、なぜ地中から金属を掘り出し続けないのでしょうか？ 兎にも角にも、これまではそれでやってこられました。実際そうなのですが、問題は持続可能性です。鉱業は最も環境を破壊する産業の一つです。国連によると、金、銅、銀などの天然資源採掘産業は、世界の炭素排出量の約

40%、生物多様性の損失の約10%の原因となっています。また、抽出費用は安定していません。過去50年間で3倍になりました。

　貴重な鉱石を見つけるのが難しくなるにつれて、掘り出す費用は高くなります。そのため、リサイクルサービスの収益性をすでに押し上げ始めています。リサイクル業者は現在、世界中で毎年約5000万トンの電子機器廃棄物が発生していることに、より大きな関心を寄せ始めています。今後は多くの中古コンピューター販売店が、喜んであなたの古いコンピューターを無料でリサイクルしてくれるでしょう。

　しかし、近い将来には、ますます競争が激しく革新的となるリサイクル業界から、より一層融通の効いたサービスが提供されるようになることが期待されます。古いパソコンや壊れたミキサーを高額のお金に換えられるときが来るかもしれません。今のところ、最高のアドバイスは、すぐにリサイクルするか、まだ行動は起こさずに新しい展開を待つことです。やってはいけないのは、何であれ電子機器関連の物をゴミとして捨ててしまうことです。

Unit
8

あともう一息です！

115

ドキュメンタリーの内容について下記の設問に答えましょう。解答と解説、翻訳はページの下にあります。

Q1 What is "urban mining"?
(A) Extracting metals from discarded gadgets
(B) Throwing used computers into landfill
(C) Recycling gold, silver and bronze Olympic medals
(D) Exchanging old computers with new ones

Q2 According to the documentary, what is the last thing you should do with electronic devices?
(A) Thow them away
(B) Expect them to be better
(C) Recycle them free of charge
(D) Dig them from the ground

解答と解説

Q1 解答（A）
「都市鉱山発掘」とは何ですか？
(A) 廃棄された電子機器から金属を抽出すること
(B) 中古のコンピューターを埋立地に捨てること
(C) オリンピックの金銀銅メダルをリサイクルすること
(D) 古いコンピューターを新品のものと代えること

解説 we should start mining the mountains of discarded gadgets instead of throwing them into landfillと言った直後に、It's called "urban mining."と続けています。

Q2 解答（A）
ドキュメンタリーによれば、電子機器についてもっともやってはいけないことは何ですか？
(A) 廃棄すること
(B) 改良されるのを期待すること
(C) 無料でリサイクルに回すこと
(D) 地中から掘り起こすこと

解説 最後の What you shouldn't do is throw anything electronic in the trash. の What you shouldn't do が設問の the last thing you should do と同じ意味。anything electronic が設問では electronic devices と言い換えられ、throw ... in the trash は throw away ...と同じ意味です。したがって、(A) が正解です。

最後に、スラッシュの箇所でリピートしてみます。かたまりごとに、意味が わかっているか確認しながら口に出してみましょう。

 18

If someone told you there was a gold mine in your backyard, / you might be tempted to pick up a shovel and start digging. // Virtually no one has such luck, / of course. // But just about every household in the industrial world / does have a store of untapped mineral resources. // Nationwide, there are billions of outdated or broken computers, printers, mobile phones / and numerous other useless gadgets and appliances lying forgotten / in closets, attics, basements and garages. //

They contain thousands of tons of valuable metals, / like copper, silver, gold and titanium. // Of course, it takes some expertise to extract that value. // The ordinary consumer might be able to locate and strip the copper wire / out of a disused electric motor, / but it takes a pro to find gold in an old computer. // With the right knowledge and equipment, however, / a recycler can extract more gold from a ton of electronic junk / than miners get from a ton of high-grade ore. //

As our phones and computers go out of date ever more quickly, / recycling advocates say / we should start mining the mountains of discarded gadgets / instead of throwing them into landfill. // It's called "urban mining," / and it works. // One demonstration of this was carried out in Japan / in the run-up to the Tokyo Olympic Games. // In a very nifty experimental program, / consumers from all over Japan / donated about 6 million old mobile phones / and 72,000 tons of other electronic trash. // Recyclers mined it, / producing enough metal / to mint about 5,000 gold, silver and bronze Olympic medals / for the Tokyo Games to be held in 2021. //

Unit
8

But why not just keep digging metal up out of the ground? // After all, it's always worked before. // That's true, but the problem is sustainability. // Mining is one of the most environmentally destructive industries around. // Natural-resource-extraction industries like gold, copper and silver mining / are responsible for about 40 percent of worldwide carbon emissions / and for about 10 percent of biodiversity loss, / according to the United Nations. // And the rate of extraction is not stable. // It has tripled over the past 50 years. //

As valuable ores become harder to find, / the cost of digging them up will increase. // That has already begun to boost the profitability / of recycling services. // Recyclers are now beginning to look / with greater interest at the roughly 50 million tons of electronic waste / produced worldwide each year. // Many used computer shops will now happily recycle your old computer / free of charge. //

But in the near future, / expect to see much more accommodating services / from an increasingly competitive / and innovative recycling industry. // The time may come / when you can exchange your old computers and broken kitchen blenders / for good money. // For now, / the best advice is to recycle immediately, / or hold and watch for new developments. // What you shouldn't do is / throw anything electronic in the trash. //

Unit
8

 古い携帯電話、どこに
やったかな？

🎧 19-21 　　　　　　　　　　　　　　　　　　　**LISTENING**

| 難易度 ●●●● 4 | 460語（やや長い） | 心理学／レクチャー | 🇺🇸 女 |

TASK

1 あなたは大学で講義を聞いています。教授の話をうまく講義メモにまとめるにはどうすればいいか考えましょう。　　[**学習目標時間30分**]

● 音声を繰り返し聞いて理論とその例を英語でメモしてください。その後、他の人に話すつもりで、講義内容を Brief summary に130語程度でまとめてみましょう。必要に応じて次ページの「単語のヘルプ」も参考にしましょう（解答例は pp. 122-123）。

🎧 19 ···◆

Introduction

Body

　・_____
　　　example(s)_____
　・_____
　　　example(s)_____
　・_____
　　　example(s)_____
　・_____
　　　example(s)_____

Closing remarks _____

Brief summary
I heard an interesting lecture today ...

_____
_____
_____
_____
_____

⌐ 単語のヘルプ ⌐

- ☐ evolution　進化
- ☐ verbal　言語による
- ☐ pervade 〜　〜に行き渡る
- ☐ scent gland　体臭腺
- ☐ secrete　分泌する
- ☐ disperse　撒き散らす
- ☐ social insect　社会性昆虫
- ☐ confrontational　対立の
- ☐ intricate　複雑な
- ☐ hive　ミツバチの巣
- ☐ lemur　キツネザル
- ☐ elaborate　精巧な
- ☐ bat a hand away　手を振り払う
- ☐ reconciliation　和解
- ☐ chimp　チンパンジー
- ☐ density　密度、濃度
- ☐ emergence　出現

Unit
9

🎧 **19** ··◆

☐ take a look at something more basic　より基本的なものを見る

☐ call these more basic forms of communication nonverbal communication　このような、より基本的なコミュニケーション形態を非言語コミュニケーションと呼ぶ

☐ common in the animal world　動物界で一般的な

☐ do all they can to make themselves look bigger　自分をより大きく見せるためにできる限りのことをする

☐ if confronted by a bear or coyote　クマやコヨーテに出くわしたら

☐ can become quite intricate and sophisticated　非常に複雑で高度なものになりえる

☐ brings about a reconciliation　和解をもたらす

☐ what their future relationship will be like　将来の関係がどうなるか

☐ effective strategies for survival　生き残るための効果的な戦略

☐ communication through facial expression　顔の表情によるコミュニケーション

TASKの解答例

Introduction
communication tools — before spoken language
Body
　　・smell
　　　[example(s)]　marking (my space, work trail, get ready to fight)
　　・visual body language
　　　[example(s)]　look bigger and powerful
　　・mechanism — intricate, sophisticated
　　　[example(s)]　bees — dances, vibration
　　　lemurs — stink
　　・gestures (chimpanzees)
　　　[example(s)]　after a fight

Closing remarks

next — facial expressions > verbal languages

Brief summary

I heard an interesting lecture in Professor Dike's class today. It was about communication before the birth of a language: nonverbal communication. The first point the professor made was that some animals communicate through the sense of smell. They leave signs that say "This is my terriroty," "Follow the trail," or "Get ready for a fight." The second type of nonverbal communication she introduced was visual body language. Animals try to make themselves look bigger and more powerful in front of their enemies. The third point she made was how complicated nonverbal communication can be. Bees use dances and wing vibrations to convey specific information to other bees. She also talked about chimpanzees. They can finish a fight and reconcile with each other just with gestures. I'm looking forward to the next lecture, where the next stage of the evolution of communication will be discussed.

日本語訳

今日、ダイク教授の授業でおもしろい講義を聞きました。テーマは、言語誕生前のコミュニケーション、つまり、非言語コミュニケーションです。教授が挙げた1つ目のポイントは、嗅覚を通して意思疎通する動物がいるということです。そうした動物は、「ここは私の陣地だ」「この道をたどれ」「戦いの準備をせよ」という意味のサインを残します。教授が紹介してくれた非言語コミュニケーションの2つ目の種類は、視覚的なボディーランゲージです。動物は敵の前では自分をより大きく、より力強く見せようとします。教授の3つ目のポイントは非言語コミュニケーションがいかに複雑になりうるかについてです。ミツバチは特定の情報を他のハチに伝えるために、ダンスや羽の振動を使います。それから、教授はチンパンジーの話もしてくれました。ジェスチャーだけで戦いをやめて仲直りすることができるとのこと。コミュニケーションにおいてその次に起きた進化について語られる次の授業が楽しみです。

Unit
9

答え合わせの後に、Brief summary の音声を聞いてみましょう。

 20

聞き取りのコツ

大学の講義などの英文が複雑なのは、修飾語句が多用されているからです。基本的な単文にいろいろな要素が加わって、より細かい内容を表しています。

● 関係詞による情報追加

関係詞を見ると、後ろから訳してみたくなりますが、which/that を「それでそれは」のように情報追加の標識ととらえれば、後戻りする必要もなくなるため、リスニングする時の理解が楽になります。who なら「それでその人(たち)は」、where なら「それでそこでは」などのように、他の関係詞にも応用できます。

many animals have special scent glands in their paws or tails, which have evolved to function as marking instruments

→ special scent glands in their paws or tails (足や尾にある特殊な体臭腺) と言ってから、which (それでそれが) とつなぎ、have evolved to function as marking instruments (進化してマーキング機能をもった) と説明を続けています。

Social insects like ants leave trails of scent that can mean ...

→ trails of scent (においの跡) と言ってから、that (それでそれが) とつなぎ、can mean ... (…というふうに言える) と、その意味するところを説明しています。

● 挿入句による情報追加

修飾される語句のあとにカンマをつけて (ない場合もある)、そのあとに修飾語句を続けます。同格の用法も含まれます。

Before we talk about verbal communication, spoken language, ...

→ verbal communication (言語によるコミュニケーション) を spoken language (話し言葉) と言い換えています。

Chimpanzees, our closest evolutionary relatives, ...

→ chimpanzees を our closest evolutionary relatives (進化上、人類にもっとも近い動物) と説明しています。

one might extend its open hand, palm up, ...

→ extend its open hand (手を差し出す) に対して、palm up (手のひらを上に向けて) と情報を追加しています。

● 後置修飾による情報追加

形容詞は必ずしも名詞 (句) の前にあるとは限りません。分詞ではよくある後置修飾の用法が、普通の形容詞にも使われます。

another nonverbal mode of communication common in the animal world

→ another nonverbal mode of communication (別のコミュニケーション形態) を common in the animal world (動物界でよくある) が後ろから修飾しています。

Tips **すぐに応用したい表現**

The odors usually indicate something like "I was here. It's my space."
→ something や someone はそれぞれ「何か」「誰か」ととらえずに、単に「もの」「人」と考えたほうがしっくり来る場合があります。An optimist is someone who expects something good in the future. を「楽観主義者とは、将来いい何かが起きると期待している誰かのことです」とすると違和感がありますね。「いいことが起きると期待している<u>人</u>のことです」ととらえたほうが自然です。

they don't come close to verbal language in terms of density of information
→ come close to ... は「…に近づく」の意味ですが、これを否定すると、「…にはとうていかなわない」という意味になります。When it comes to math, I don't come close to him. (数学のこととなると、僕は彼の足元にも及ばない) のように使えます。

では英文を見ながら、もう一度、聞きましょう。

 19 ....◆

In today's lecture, we're going to talk about communication and particularly about how the evolution of communication has equipped us with the communicative tools we use every day. Before we talk about verbal communication, spoken language, I'd like to take a look at something more basic. Living things have been communicating in simpler ways since long before anyone could speak.

We call these more basic forms of communication nonverbal communication, and they absolutely pervade interactions among animals. One very basic channel of nonverbal communication is through the sense of smell. For instance, many animals have special scent glands in their paws or tails, which have evolved to function as marking instruments. These glands secrete aromatic substances that can be dispersed in air or water, or applied to surfaces. The odors usually indicate something like "I was here. It's my space." Social insects like ants leave trails of scent that can mean something like "Work trail" or "Get ready to fight."

Visual body language is another nonverbal mode of communication common in the animal world. Animals in a confrontational situation often do all they can to make themselves look bigger and more powerful. I was on a forest hike once, and my guide told me what to do if confronted by a bear or coyote. "First, try to look big," he said. He suggested holding up my coat or backpack and waving my arms in the air. The simple message here is, "I am big. I'm dangerous." The guide said it works —— sometimes.

Nonverbal communication mechanisms like smell, body movement and sounds or vibrations, can become quite intricate and sophisticated. Bees, for instance, fly in specific meaningful patterns called "dances." The vibrations from their wings communicate the location of flowers to others in the hive. And lemurs engage in "stink fights." They wipe scent from wrist glands onto their tails and then wave their tails and each other in a contest for dominance through smell.

Chimpanzees, our closest evolutionary relatives, engage in very elaborate and meaningful gestural communication. After a fight between two chimpanzees, for example, one might extend its open hand, palm up, toward the other. The other may bat the hand away, or gently touch it, or even kiss it. This can start a series of mutual gesturing that brings about a reconciliation. Without a word, the two chimps decide whether to stop fighting and what their future relationship will be like.

These nonverbal modes of communication are effective strategies for survival. But they don't come close to verbal language in terms of density of information, complexity of meaning or nuance. In our next talk, we're going to look at the evolution of communication through facial expression. We'll discuss theories about its relationship to the emergence of verbal prehistoric language.

Unit 9

日本語訳

今日の講義では、コミュニケーションについて、特にコミュニケーションの進化が私たちが日常的に使用しているコミュニケーションツールをどのように私たちにもたらしてきたかについて話します。言葉のコミュニケーション、つまり、話し言葉について話す前に、より基本的なことを見ておきたいと思います。生物は人間が話すことができるようになるずっと前から、より簡単な方法でコミュニケーションをとってきました。

このようなより基本的なコミュニケーション形態は非言語コミュニケーションと呼び、動物間の相互作用に深く関わっています。非言語コミュニケーションの極めて基本的な経路の一つは、嗅覚を通して行なわれるものです。たとえば、多くの動物は足や尾に特殊な体臭腺を持っており、それが進化してマーキング手段として機能するようになりました。こうした腺は、空気中や水中に散布したり、表面に付着したりする芳香物質を分泌します。そのにおいは通常、「私はここにいました。それは私のスペースです」といったことを示すものです。アリのような社会性昆虫は、「この道をたどれ」や「戦う準備をせよ」などの意味を表しうるにおいの痕跡を残します。

視覚的ボディランゲージが、動物界で一般的な非言語的コミュニケーションのもう一つの方法です。対立的な状況にある動物はよく、自らをより大きく、より強く見せるためにできる限りのことをします。私は一度森にハイキングに行ったことがありますが、ガイドさんがクマやコヨーテに出くわしたらどうすればいいかを教えてくれました。「まず自分自身を大きく見せようとしてください」と彼は言いました。自分の上着やバックパックを持ち上げ、腕を宙に振るよう提案しました。ここでの単純なメッセージは、「私は大きいですよ。私は危険ですよ」というものです。そのガイドさんによると、これはうまくいくとのことです。時々ですが。

嗅覚、体の動き、音や振動などの非言語的なコミュニケーション方法は、非常に複雑で高度なものになることがあります。たとえば、ミツバチは「ダンス」と呼ばれる特定の意味を表すパターンで飛

びます。羽の出す振動は、花の位置を巣にいる仲間に伝えます。また、キツネザルは「悪臭合戦」を行います。彼らは手首の腺のにおいを拭き取って尻尾につけ、互いに相手に向かってその尻尾を振って、においを通した優位性を競うのです。

　チンパンジーはヒトの進化上の最近縁種であり、非常に精巧で意味のある身振りを使ったコミュニケーションを行なっています。たとえば、2匹のチンパンジーがけんかをした後、一方のチンパンジーが開いた手を、手のひらを上に向けて、もう一方のチンパンジーに対して伸ばします。もう一方はその手を振り払うしぐさをしたり、それにそっと触ったり、ときにはキスをしたりすることもあります。これが互いに身振りを交わし、和解をもたらすこととなる一連の行為の始まりとなりえます。一言も発することなく、この2匹のチンパンジーはけんかをやめるかどうか、そして将来の関係がどうなるかを決めるのです。

　このような非言語的コミュニケーション方法は、生存のために効果的な戦略です。しかし、情報の密度、意味の複雑さ、ニュアンスといった点では、言語にはとうてい及びません。次の講義では、顔の表情によるコミュニケーションの進化について見ていきます。そのことと有史以前の言語の出現との関係についての様々な学説について論じる予定です。

5 講義の内容について下記の設問に答えましょう。解答と解説、翻訳はページの下にあります。

Q1 In the lecture, which of the following is NOT mentioned as a means of nonverbal communication?
(A) The sense of smell
(B) Visual body language
(C) Facial expressions
(D) Complexity of meanings

Q2 What kind of communication do chimpanzees engage in?
(A) Dances
(B) Stink fights
(C) Gestures
(D) Verbal language

解答と解説

Q1 解答（D）
講義の中で非言語コミュニケーションの手段として取り上げられていないのは、次のうちどれですか？
(A) 嗅覚   (C) 顔の表情
(B) 視覚的ボディランゲージ   (D) 意味の複雑さ

解説 (A) は One very basic channel of nonverbal communication is through the sense of smell. で、(B) は Visual body language is another nonverbal mode of communication … で、(C) は we're going to look at the evolution of communication through facial expression で触れられています。complexity of meaning は they don't come close to verbal language in terms of density of information, complexity of meaning, … と言語が果たす役割の一つとして述べられているだけなので、正解は (D) です。

Unit
9

Q2 解答（C）
チンパンジーはどのようなコミュニケーション手段を取りますか？
(A) 踊り   (C) 身振り
(B) におい合戦   (D) 言語

解説 チンパンジーに関しては、Chimpanzees, our closest evolutionary relatives, engage in very elaborate and meaningful gestural communication. と述べられているので、ジェスチャーを使って意思疎通をしていることがわかります。したがって、正解は (C) です。

最後に、スラッシュの箇所でリピートしてみます。かたまりごとに、意味が
わかっているか確認しながら口に出してみましょう。

🎧 21 .... ◆

In today's lecture, / we're going to talk about communication / and particularly about how the evolution of communication has equipped us / with the communicative tools we use every day. // Before we talk about verbal communication, spoken language, / I'd like to take a look at something more basic. // Living things have been communicating in simpler ways / since long before anyone could speak. //

We call these more basic forms of communication nonverbal communication, / and they absolutely pervade interactions among animals. // One very basic channel of nonverbal communication is / through the sense of smell. // For instance, many animals have special scent glands / in their paws or tails, / which have evolved to function as marking instruments. // These glands secrete aromatic substances / that can be dispersed in air or water, or applied to surfaces. // The odors usually indicate something like / "I was here. It's my space." // Social insects like ants leave trails of scent / that can mean something like / "Work trail" or "Get ready to fight." //

Visual body language is another nonverbal mode of communication / common in the animal world. // Animals in a confrontational situation often do all they can / to make themselves look bigger and more powerful. // I was on a forest hike once, / and my guide told me what to do / if confronted by a bear or coyote. // "First, try to look big," he said. // He suggested holding up my coat or backpack / and waving my arms in the air. // The simple message here is, / "I am big. I'm dangerous." // The guide said it works — sometimes. //

Nonverbal communication mechanisms / like smell, body movement, and sounds or vibrations, / can become quite intricate and sophisticated. // Bees, for instance, / fly in specific meaningful patterns called "dances." // The vibrations from their wings / communicate the location of flowers to others in the hive. // And lemurs engage in "stink fights." // They wipe scent from wrist glands onto their tails, / and then wave their tails at each other / in a contest for dominance through smell. //

Chimpanzees, our closest evolutionary relatives, / engage in very elaborate and meaningful gestural communication. // After a fight between two chimpanzees, for example, / one might extend its open hand, palm up, toward the other. // The other may bat the hand away, / or gently touch it, / or even kiss it. // This can start a series of mutual gesturing / that brings about a reconciliation. // Without a word, / the two chimps decide whether to stop fighting, / and what their future relationship will be like. //

These nonverbal modes of communication / are effective strategies for survival. // But they don't come close to verbal language / in terms of density of information, / complexity of meaning, or nuance. // In our next talk, / we're going to look at the evolution of communication through facial expression. // We'll discuss theories about its relationship / to the emergence of verbal prehistoric language. //

Unit
9

22-24

LISTENING

難易度 ●●●●● 5 | 430語（やや長い） | 医学／ニュース特集 男

 TASK

1 ニュースを聞いて、数字を含め、内容を正確に聞き取りましょう。

[学習目標時間25分]

● 音声を聞いて、それぞれの数字が示していることを空欄に書きましょう。また、内容を誤解している友人の発言を次のトラックで聞き、適切に修正してください。音声は何度聞いてもかまいません。必要に応じて次ページの「単語のヘルプ」も参考にしましょう（解答例は pp. 135-136）。

🎧 **22** ....◆

A. 数字の聞き取り

1. nearly 30 percent _____

2. 0.4 percent _____

3. 1.7 percent _____

4. just under 1 percent _____

5. 5 percent _____

6. 1.7 million _____

7. 600,000 _____

8. more than 4,500 _____

9. more than 1,600 _____

🎧 **23** ....◆

B. 発言内容の修正

Question 1 _____

Question 2 _____

Question 3 _____

Question 4 _____

Question 5 _____

(単語のヘルプ)

- [ ] elusive　見つけられない
- [ ] nuisance　厄介者（ここでは病気のこと）
- [ ] deadliness　死亡率
- [ ] lethality　致死率
- [ ] prevention　予防
- [ ] killer　死因
- [ ] eliminate　除去する
- [ ] detect　検知する
- [ ] clinical research　臨床研究
- [ ] gene therapy　遺伝子療法
- [ ] immune system　免疫系
- [ ] chemotherapy　化学療法
- [ ] case　患者
- [ ] translate into 〜　（換算すると）〜となる
- [ ] infancy　初期段階

Unit
10

🎧 22 ....◆

☐ remains elusive　いまだにはっきりはしていない

☐ the deadliness of the disease　その病気の死亡率

☐ decrease in cancer lethality　がんによる死亡率の低下

☐ better prevention and better treatment　予防と治療の進歩

☐ detect lung cancers earlier　肺がんをより早期に発見する

☐ progress in clinical research　臨床研究の進歩

☐ contributing to improved outcomes　結果の改善に寄与している

☐ it's fair to say ...　…と言ってもいい

☐ the glass is half full　コップには水が半分満ちている（the glass is half empty に対して、前向きな見方をすることを表す表現）

TASK の解答例

それぞれの数字が何を示しているかを把握することが大事です。また、千の位以上は日本語と区切りが異なるため、より注意して聞く必要があります。

A. 数字の聞き取り

1. nearly 30 percent　　　過去30年のがん致死率減少割合
   → the nationwide death rate from cancer has declined by <u>nearly 30 percent</u> over the past 30 years

2. 0.4 percent　　　　　　（かつての）がんによる死亡者数の前年比減少割合
   → the number of people nationwide who died of cancer was <u>0.4 percent</u> less than in the previous year

3. 1.7 percent　　　　　　昨年と比較した場合の上記減少割合
   → That compares with an annual decrease of <u>1.7 percent</u> last year.

4. just under 1 percent　　30年前の肺がんによる死者数の年間減少割合
   → the number of deaths from lung cancer was decreasing at an annual rate of <u>just under 1 percent</u> 30 years ago

5. 5 percent　　　　　　　昨年と比較した場合の上記割合
   → compared with <u>5 percent</u> last year

6. 1.7 million　　　　　　今後1年間の全国でのがん発症予想患者数
   → a total of <u>1.7 million</u> new cases of all types of cancer ... are expected nationwide during the coming year

7. 600,000　　　　　　　今後1年間の全国でのがんによる予想死者数
   → <u>600,000</u> deaths, are expected nationwide during the coming year

8. more than 4,500　　　一日換算した場合の上記患者数
   → That translates into <u>more than 4,500</u> new cases each day

9. more than 1,600　　　一日換算した場合の上記死者数
   → That translates into ... <u>more than 1,600</u> deaths each day

B. 発言内容の修正

友人の発言を、次（You）のように修正できるといいでしょう。

Question 1

Friend: I heard that a reliable cure for cancer has been discovered.（信頼の置けるがん治療法が見つかったと聞きましたが）

You: Not really. It's still elusive. But modern medical science has reduced the overall harm from the disease.（実際には違います。まだわかっていません。ただ、現代の医学の力でその病気による全般的な害は減りました）

Question 2

Friend: The cancer survival rate is still low, isn't it?（がん生存率はいまだに低いのですね？）

You: On the contrary. The latest report is full of good news.（その逆です。最新の報告にはいいニュースばかりが載っていますよ）

Question 3

Friend: The national death rate from the diseases has decreased to about 30 percent over the past 30 years, right?（その病気による全国的な致死率は、過去30年間で約30％にまで減ったのですね？）

You: Well, it says the rate is down *by* 30 percent, not *to* 30 percent.（実際には、30％の減少であって、30％に減少したわけではありません）

Question 4

Friend: Thirty years ago, the number of people who died from cancer was 0.4 percent less, compared to last year. Am I correct?（30年前は昨年に比べて、がんで死亡した人は0.4％少なかった。それで合っていますか？）

You: Compared to the previous year, to be precise.（正確には、その前年と比較した場合です）

Question 5

Friend: I understand there used to be 1.7 million new cases of cancer and 60,000 deaths each year.（かつては毎年170万人の新規がん患者が出て、6万人が亡くなっているということですね）

You: Unfortunately, we still have 1.7 million new cases and 600,000 —— not 60,000 deaths now, which means over 4,500 people contract cancer and over 1,600 people die every day.（残念ながら、いまの時点で170万人の患者が出て、6万人ではなく60万人が亡くなっています。つまり、毎日4,500人を超える方々ががんにかかり、1,600人を超える方々が亡くなっていることになります）

3 聞き取りのコツ

難しい単語と違って、やさしい単語は「知っている」という安心感からあまり頭に残らないもの。実際にはその本当の意味を取り損なっているかもしれません。

● 指示代名詞が指すもの

「that＝それ」だけでなく、具体的な内容の理解が大事であることは言うまでもありません。また、this は近くの物事を、that は少し離れた物事を指すという違いがありますが、話の流れから明らかなことには、直近であっても that が使われます。

That compares with an annual decrease of 1.7 percent last year.

→直前の0.4 percent less than in the previous year を指しています。

That translates into more than 4,500 new cases and more than 1,600 deaths each day.

→やはり直前の1.7 million new cases of all types of cancer, and 600,000 deaths を指しています。

● 冠詞や前置詞の有無

冠詞の有無で意味は変わります。

0.4 percent less than in the previous year

の the previous year（そこから見て前の年＝前年）と

decrease of 1.7 percent last year

の last year（今年から見た前の年＝昨年）を混同しないようにしましょう。前者は the last year と表現される場合もあります。

また、has declined by nearly 30 percent のように増減について述べるときも、

increased/decreased (by) XX（XXの分だけ増加する／減少する）

increased/decreased to XX（XXの値まで増加する／減少する）

の両者を取り違いがちです。by は省略されることがあります。冠詞も前置詞も短い単語なので、聞き逃しには気をつけましょう。

● 昔ながらの言い回し、ことわざ

コップに水が半分入った状態を「まだ半分ある (The glass is half full.)」ととるか、「もう半分しかない (The glass is half empty.)」ととるかによって、物事の見方が楽観的か悲観的かがわかると言われます。最後の、

the glass is half full, rather than half empty

はその定説を応用したものです。話の中で比喩としてよく使われます。

Unit
10

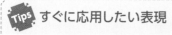 すぐに応用したい表現

Both of these factors have been clearly evident in the trends in lung cancer, which is the No. 1 killer among all cancers.

→このkillerは「人を殺すもの」、つまり、「死因」のこと。このように動詞や名詞に-erを付けるだけで、難しいと思っていた意味合いが簡単に表せる場合があります。また、walker(歩行器)、hatter(帽子販売人)だけでなく、frequent flyer(よく飛行機を利用する人)やgame changer(形勢を一変させるもの)のように他の単語とともに使われるものにも注目しましょう。

On the bright side, however, the numbers show that these figures are expected to continue to decrease ...

→ on the bright side で「物事の明るい面としては、長所としては」の意味。暗い面を(on the dark side)見ている人に対しては、Why don't you look on the brighter side of things? のように言えます。

... it's fair to say the glass is half full, rather than half empty.

→ fair は That's not fair! の言い回しでよく使われます。「それはないよ」といったニュアンスです。ここでは It's fair to say ... で「…と言ってもいいでしょう」の意味。いずれも「公平な」と訳してしまうとややぎこちなくなってしまう単語です。

4 では英文を見ながら、もう一度、聞きましょう。

🎧 22

Despite more than a century of research, a reliable cure for cancer remains elusive. But a recent study by the Center for Advanced Cancer Research, at Ainsworth Medical University, shows that modern medical science is achieving the next best thing: reducing the overall harm done by the disease. Even if a simple cure is never found, the study suggests that cancer might someday be reduced to a treatable nuisance, like the common cold.

According to the study, the deadliness of the disease is steadily decreasing each year as treatments improve. In fact, the nationwide death rate from cancer has declined by nearly 30 percent over the past 30 years. And that progress is speeding up. The annual rate of decrease in cancer lethality increases every year. In the first year of the study, 30 years ago, the number of people nationwide who died of cancer was 0.4 percent less than in the previous year. That compares with an annual decrease of 1.7 percent last year.

The report indicates that the main factors in the decline in the death rate are better prevention and better treatment. Both of these factors have been clearly evident in the trends in lung cancer, which is the No. 1 killer among all cancers. Nationwide, the number of deaths from lung cancer was decreasing at an annual rate of just under 1 percent 30 years ago, compared with 5 percent last year. Experts say that a decrease in smoking and progress in eliminating asbestos dust from the environment have been major factors in prevention.

As with breast cancer, improvements in medical imaging technology and public awareness have also helped doctors detect lung cancers earlier, when they are more likely to be successfully treated. In addition to early detection, progress in clinical research is bringing more effective treatments to market. Each year, advances in gene therapy provide doctors with more useful options in stimulating the body's

Unit
10

own immune system to fight lung cancers. More advanced surgical procedures and better chemotherapy, radiation therapy and combinations of treatments are also contributing to improved outcomes.

Despite all this progress, a total of 1.7 million new cases of all types of cancer, and 600,000 deaths, are expected nationwide during the coming year. That translates into more than 4,500 new cases and more than 1,600 deaths each day. On the bright side, however, the numbers show that these figures are expected to continue to decrease as ever-more lives are saved by early detection and better treatment. Given that advanced technologies like gene therapy are still in their infancy, it's fair to say the glass is half full, rather than half empty.

日本語訳

1世紀を超える研究が行われてきたにもかかわらず、がんの確実な治療法はまだつかみどころがない状態のままです。しかしエインズワース医科大学のがん先端研究センターによる最近の研究では、現代の医学は次善を達成しつつあり、それはつまり、この病気による全体的な害を減らすことです。たとえ純然たる治療法が見つからなくても、いつかがんが風邪のような治療可能な厄介な病気になると、その研究は示唆しています。

その研究によると、この病気の死亡率は、治療法が改善するにつれて、毎年着実に減少しています。実際のところ、全国のがんによる死亡率は、過去30年間で30%近く減少しました。さらに、その進歩は加速しています。がん死亡率の年間減少率は毎年上がっています。研究の初年度である30年前には、全国のがんによる死亡者数は前年比で0.4%の減少でした。それに比べ、昨年からは年間1.7%減少しています。

その報告によると、死亡率の減少の主な要因は予防と治療の進歩です。この2つの要因は、すべてのがんの中で死因1位である肺がんの動向から明らかです。全国的に見ると、肺がんによる死亡者数は、30年前は年率1%をやや下回るほどの減少で、それに対して昨年は5%でした。専門家は、喫煙の減少と環境からのアスベスト粉塵の除去の進歩が、予防の主な要因になったとしています。

乳がんと同様に、医療画像技術と一般の意識の向上も、治療が成功する可能性がより高い早期に医師が肺がんを発見することに役立ちました。早期発見に加えて、臨床研究の進歩がより効果的な治療法を医療現場にもたらしています。毎年、遺伝子治療の進歩により、医師は肺がんと闘うために体が本来持っている免疫系を刺激する有用な選択肢を手にしています。より進歩した外科的処置とより優れた化学療法、放射線療法、そしてそうした治療法の併用も、結果の改善に寄与しています。

このような進歩にもかかわらず、今後1年間で全種類のがんを合わせて合計170万人が新たに発症し、60万人が死亡すると予想されています。換算すると、毎日4,500人を超す患者が新たに発生し、1,600人を超す人々が死亡することになります。しかし、明るい面としては、こうした数字は、患者数および死亡者数がこれまで通り減少し続けること、つまり、早期発見とより良い治療によって、救われる命が今まで以上に増えるということを示しています。遺伝子治療のような先端技術がまだ初期段階にあることを考えると、コップは半分空なのではなく、半分満たされていると言ってもいいでしょう。

Unit
10

5 ニュース特集の内容について下記の設問に答えましょう。解答と解説、翻訳はページの下にあります。

Q1 What does "achieving the next best thing" mean?
  (A) Finding a reliable cure for cancer
  (B) Reducing the overall harm from cancer
  (C) Decreasing the death rate to zero
  (D) Compiling statistics on cancer survival

Q2 What has NOT greatly contributed to the fewer deaths of cancer?
  (A) Gene therapy
  (B) The elimination of asbestos
  (C) Early detection
  (D) Better surgical skills

解答と解説

Q1 解答（B）
「次善を達成する」とはどういう意味ですか？
(A) 信頼のおけるがん治療法を発見すること
(B) がんによる全体的な害を減少させること
(C) 致死率をゼロまで減らすこと
(D) がん生存率の統計をまとめること

解説 the next best thingとは最善ではないがその次に良いとされることを表します。ここでは直後にreducing the overall harm done by the disease（その病気による全体的な害を減らすこと）と説明されています。したがって(B)が正解です。

Q2 解答（A）
がんによる死亡者数の減少に大きく寄与してこなかったことは何ですか？
(A) 遺伝子治療　　　　(B) アスベスト除去
(C) 早期発見　　　　　(D) 手術技術向上

解説 (B)についてはprogress in eliminating asbestos dust from the environment have been major factors in preventionと、(C)についてはIn addition to early detection, progress in clinical research is bringing more effective treatmentsと、(D)についてはMore advanced surgical procedures ... are also contributing to improved outcomes.と述べられています。遺伝子治療はadvanced technologies like gene therapy are still in their infancyから、その技術がまだ初期段階にあるとわかり、大きく貢献しているわけではないので、正解は(A)です。

最後に、スラッシュの箇所でリピートしてみます。かたまりごとに、意味が
わかっているか確認しながら口に出してみましょう。

 24

Despite more than a century of research, / a reliable cure for cancer remains elusive. // But a recent study by the Center for Advanced Cancer Research, / at Ainsworth Medical University, / shows that modern medical science is achieving the next best thing: / reducing the overall harm done by the disease. // Even if a simple cure is never found, / the study suggests that / cancer might some day be reduced to a treatable nuisance, / like the common cold. //

According to the study, / the deadliness of the disease is steadily decreasing each year / as treatments improve. // In fact, the nationwide death rate from cancer / has declined by nearly 30 percent / over the past 30 years. // And that progress is speeding up. // The annual rate of decrease in cancer lethality increases every year. // In the first year of the study, / 30 years ago, / the number of people nationwide who died of cancer / was 0.4 percent less than in the previous year. // That compares with an annual decrease of 1.7 percent last year. //

The report indicates that / the main factors in the decline in the death rate / are better prevention and better treatment. // Both of these factors have been / clearly evident in the trends in lung cancer, / which is the No. 1 killer among all cancers. // Nationwide, the number of deaths from lung cancer was decreasing / at an annual rate of just under 1 percent 30 years ago, / compared with 5 percent last year. // Experts say that a decrease in smoking / and progress in eliminating asbestos dust from the environment / have been major factors in prevention. //

Unit
10

As with breast cancer, / improvements in medical imaging technology and public awareness / have also helped doctors detect lung cancers earlier, / when they are more likely to be successfully treated. // In addition to early detection, / progress in clinical research is bringing more effective treatments to market. / Each year, / advances in gene therapy provide doctors / with more useful options in stimulating the body's own immune system / to fight lung cancers. // More advanced surgical procedures / and better chemotherapy, radiation therapy and combinations of treatments / are also contributing to improved outcomes. //

Despite all this progress, / a total of 1.7 million new cases of all types of cancer, and 600,000 deaths, / are expected nationwide during the coming year. // That translates into more than 4,500 new cases / and more than 1,600 deaths each day. // On the bright side, however, / the numbers show that these figures are expected to continue to decrease / as ever-more lives are saved by early detection and better treatment. // Given that advanced technologies / like gene therapy are still in their infancy, / it's fair to say the glass is half full, / rather than half empty. //

Unit
10

リスニング・パートはここまで。
よく頑張りました！

Go for it!

Reading を鍛える！

Chapter 3
読んだ情報を相手に伝える　基礎編

それではリーディングの Chapter です。自然な英語を素材にしているため、時々出てくる難しい単語や見慣れない言い回しに、資格試験の英文だけに慣れている人には、意外とハードルが高く感じられるかもしれません。まずは TASK に答えられるよう、読み進めましょう。

Unit 11　新しい駐輪場
〈新設備／案内〉

Unit 12　冷たい物も温かい物も
〈仕様書／説明・解説〉

Unit 13　オンライン口座を開くには
〈サービス利用開始／説明・解説〉

Unit 14　ジムの利用法
〈器具の使い方／説明・解説〉

Unit 15　新しい生活を始める
〈物件紹介／案内〉

ここからリーディングパート。
まず英文を読んでみます。

Unit 11 — 新しい駐輪場

 25-26

READING

難易度 ●● ● ● **2** ｜ 約300語（ふつう） ｜ 新設備／案内

> **1** あなたは新しい駐輪場のお知らせを読みます。その内容を、駐輪場が少ないと不平を言っていた友人に手短に伝えましょう。[**学習目標時間20分**]

● まず、以下の英文を3分を目標に読んでみましょう。次ページの「単語のヘルプ」も、必要に応じて参考にしてください。

TRIPLE-MET Makes Bike-and-Ride Easier Than Ever!

The Tri-Cities Metropolitan Rail System, TRIPLE-MET, has now completed its construction of Bike-and-Rail bicycle-parking facilities at all Bike-and-Rail centers. Now you can safely park your bicycle in covered, secure parking areas conveniently located near the entrances of major stations on the TRIPLE-MET railway system linking the cities of Bellmont, Ridgeway and Shorecrest.

To use the Bike-and-Rail system, simply visit the TRIPLE-MET website or download our convenient smartphone app. Follow the directions under the Bike-and-Rail tab to get your Bike-and-Rail User Pass. It's free for any existing TRIPLE-MET user with a Commuter Pass, Student Pass, Senior Pass or Multi-Ticket and available for an affordable fee to guest users.

Bike-and-Rail is more than just bicycle parking. Here are some of the convenient things you can do with a Bike-and-Rail pass:

- Transport your bicycle on any TRIPLE-MET bus equipped with a bicycle rack.
- Park your bicycle at any TRIPLE-MET Park-and-Ride or Bike-and-Ride hub station in a secure, locked, CCTV-monitored bicycle parking area (80 percent of stations are now equipped, with plans to expand to all stations by 2026).
- Take your bicycle on the train during non-commuter hours when conditions permit.

149

In addition to easy access to bicycle parking facilities, your Bike-and-Rail User Pass also gives you priority access to the GreenBike public bicycle share program. Use your pass when you check out a GreenBike from any of the conveniently located GreenBike locking stations and receive a 50 percent discount off the $1 GreenBike unlock fee. It's just one more reason to go two-wheeled in the Tri-Cities!

Try TRIPLE-MET Bike-and-Rail today!

(単語のヘルプ)

他にもわからないものがあったら辞書で調べて書き足しておきましょう。

☐ facility 施設

☐ covered 屋根のある

☐ conveniently located 便利なところにある

☐ app アプリ

☐ directions 指示、説明

☐ existing 既存の、現行の

☐ affordable （値段が）手ごろな

☐ equipped with～ ～が備わった

☐ hub 中心

☐ CCTV-monitored CCTVで監視された ＊CCTVは closed-circuit television［閉回路テレビ、有線テレビ］の略

☐ permit 許す

☐ priority 優先

☐ check out 借りる、借り出す

☐ unlock 開錠、ロック解除

☐ go two-wheeled 二輪車で移動する

TASK

2 あなたは読んだ内容を伝えるため、まずメモをとりました。次に、友人に電話をしましたが、相手が電話に出なかったので、メモをもとに伝言を残すことにしました。下の欄に、英語でメモと伝言内容を書いてみましょう（解答例は p. 152）。

メモ

_____

_____

_____

_____

_____

伝言内容

_____

_____

_____

_____

_____

メモ
TRIPLE-MET
new bike parking
covered, safe
near major stations
web, app > user pass
= free for present users, reasonable for guests also
- carry bikes on bus
- park in safe, locked, CCTV area (80% stations)
- take trains w/ bike

伝言内容

Hello. Tom here. I'm calling because I want to share with you some information I've just read. It's about the new bike-parking system. You are always complaining about the lack of bike-parking facilities and how sometimes you have no choice but to leave your bike on the street. I've got some great news for you! The new bike-parking lots have all now been completed, and if you are a TRIPLE-MET user, they're actually free. Visit the TRIPLE-MET website and see how to register. As well as parking your bike in a safe, locked, monitored area, you can transport it on an equipped bus or take it on a train during off-peak hours. It's good, isn't it?

日本語訳

もしもし、トムだよ。さっき読んだ情報を君にも教えたくて電話したんだ。新しい駐輪場のことなんだけど。駐輪場が少ないから、時々しかたなく道路に自転車をとめていることにいつも不満を言っているよね。いい知らせがあるよ！　新しい駐輪場がすべて完成して、TRIPLE-MET利用者なら、実質、無料なんだ。TRIPLE-METのウェブサイトを見て、登録方法をチェックしてみて。安全で施錠機能と監視カメラがついた場所にとめられるだけじゃなくて、自転車を設備付きのバスで運んだり、それに、混雑していない時間帯は電車に自転車を乗せられるんだ。いいでしょ？

答え合わせのあとに、伝言内容を音声でも聞いてみましょう。

 25 ⋯⋯⋯⋯⋯⋯⋯⋯⋯⋯⋯⋯⋯⋯⋯⋯⋯⋯⋯⋯⋯⋯⋯⋯⋯⋯⋯⋯⋯⋯⋯⋯⋯⋯⋯⋯⋯◆

3 読み方のコツ

● 並列

並列とは、A and/or B、A, B and/or(,) C、A, B, C and/or(,) D…のように2つ以上の語句を並べる表現方法です。並列には次のような特徴があります。

1. 並ぶ要素はすべて同じ構造にする

   品詞をそろえる、すべて …ing形にするなど、同列のものが並ばなければなりません。Aが動詞でBが名詞などの組み合わせは原則としてありません。

2. それぞれの要素の長さが異なる場合が多い

   Tokyo, Osaka and Fukuoka のように単語1語が並ぶ場合だけでなく、第2段落4〜6行目の

   free for any existing TRIPLE-MET user with a Commuter Pass, Student Pass, Senior Pass or Multi-Ticket

   と

   available for an affordable fee to guest users

   のように、長さがまったく違うことも多いので、読みながらどこまでがひとつの要素なのかを判断する必要があります。

3. 最後の要素の前に and または or を入れる

   A and B and C ではなく、A, B and C とするのが標準的です。and や or の前にカンマがない場合もあります。また、第1段落4行目の

   covered, secure

   や、箇条書き第2項目の

   secure, locked, CCTV-monitored

   のように、名詞または名詞句 (ここでは bicycle parking area) の前に付く形容詞が、カンマだけでつながっている場合もあります。

● 後置修飾

名詞の前ではなく、うしろに修飾語句が続く用法です。形としては、次の2種類があります。

1. 「名詞＋分詞 (句)」

   現在分詞が続く場合と過去分詞が続く場合があります。第1段落最後の

   the TRIPLE-MET railway system linking the cities of Bellmont, Ridgeway and Shorecrest

   では、linking … Shorecrest が the TRIPLE-MET railway system を、箇条書き第1項目の

   any TRIPLE-MET bus equipped with a bicycle rack

   では、equipped with a bicycle rack が any TRIPLE-MET bus を修飾して

います。なお、「分詞が1語の場合は名詞の前、2語以上なら名詞のうしろ」という基本ルールを習ったかもしれませんが、people involved (関係者) のように、1語でもうしろに付く場合があります。

2. 「名詞+形容詞 (句)」
    「名詞+関係代名詞句 (形容詞を含む)」ならわかりやすいのですが、名詞の直後に形容詞が続くこともあります (Unit 15参照)。

 Bike-and-Rail

bikeには「自転車」と「オートバイ」の意味があり、文脈からどちらであるかを判断しなければなりませんが、ここでは前者です。railは電車や列車のこと。Bike-and-Railは自宅から自転車で駅まで行き、そこから電車や列車に乗ることを指します。これに対し、駅までは奥さんか旦那さんに送ってもらい、別れ際にキスをしてから鉄道に乗り換えるというKiss-and-Rideもあります。環境によりやさしく、健康にもよい通勤方法として、今後Bike-and-Railが増えていくことでしょう。

よりよく英文を理解するために音声を使って学びます。ポーズの箇所で、意味を考えながら、繰り返し□に出してみましょう。

🔊 26 ·· ◆

TRIPLE-MET Makes Bike-and-Ride Easier Than Ever! //

The Tri-Cities Metropolitan Rail System, TRIPLE-MET, / has now completed its construction / of Bike-and-Rail bicycle-parking facilities / at all Bike-and-Rail centers. // Now you can safely park your bicycle / in covered, secure parking areas / conveniently located near the entrances of major stations / on the TRIPLE-MET railway system / linking the cities of Bellmont, Ridgeway and Shorecrest. //

To use the Bike-and-Rail system, / simply visit the TRIPLE-MET website / or download our convenient smartphone app. // Follow the directions under the Bike-and-Rail tab / to get your Bike-and-Rail User Pass. // It's free for any existing TRIPLE-MET user / with a Commuter Pass, Student Pass, Senior Pass or Multi-Ticket / and available for an affordable fee to guest users. //

Bike-and-Rail is more than just bicycle parking. // Here are some of the convenient things you can do / with a Bike-and-Rail pass: //

- Transport your bicycle / on any TRIPLE-MET bus / equipped with a bicycle rack. //
- Park your bicycle at any TRIPLE-MET Park-and-Ride / or Bike-and-Ride hub station / in a secure, locked, CCTV-monitored bicycle parking area / (80 percent of stations are now equipped, / with plans to expand to all stations by 2026). //
- Take your bicycle on the train / during non-commuter hours / when conditions permit. //

In addition to easy access to bicycle parking facilities, / your Bike-and-Rail User Pass also gives you / priority access to the GreenBike public bicycle share program. // Use your pass / when you check out a GreenBike / from any of the conveniently located GreenBike locking stations / and receive a 50 percent discount off the $1 GreenBike unlock fee. // It's just one more reason / to go two-wheeled in the Tri-Cities! //

Try TRIPLE-MET Bike-and-Rail today! //

TRIPLE-MET でバイク＆ライドのご利用を今まで以上に簡単に！

　トライシティーズ・メトロポリタン・レール・システム (TRIPLE-MET) は、すべてのバイク＆レールセンターにバイク＆レール用駐輪場を建設し終えました。これにより、ベルモント市、リッジウェイ市、ショアクレスト市を結ぶ TRIPLE-MET 鉄道システムの主要駅の入り口付近に設置された、利便性の高い屋根付で安全な自転車置き場に、安心して自転車をとめることができます。

　バイク＆レールシステムを利用するためには、TRIPLE-MET のウェブサイトへのアクセスか、当社の便利なスマートフォンアプリのダウンロードだけですみます。「バイク＆レール」と書かれたタブの下の指示に従って、バイク＆レールユーザーパスを入手してください。TRIPLE-MET の既存ユーザーで、コミューターパス、スチューデントパス、シニアパス、マルチチケットをお持ちの方は無料で、また、不定期利用者の方には手ごろな料金でご利用いただけます。

　バイク＆レールは単なる駐輪サービスではありません。ここでは、バイク＆レールパスを持っているとできる便利なことのいくつかを紹介します。

- 自転車用ラックを装備した TRIPLE-MET バスで自転車を輸送すること。
- TRIPLE-MET パーク＆ライドまたはバイク＆ライドのハブステーションの、安全で施錠機能を備えた、CCTV 監視付きの自転車置き場（現在 80% の駅に整備されており、2026 年までに全駅に拡大予定）のどこにでも自転車をとめること。
- 条件が許せば、通勤時間帯外に自転車を電車内に持ち込むこと。

　駐輪施設へのアクセスが容易であることに加え、バイク＆レールのユーザーパスでグリーンバイク公共自転車共有プログラムを優先的に利用することもできます。便利な場所にあるグリーンバイク施錠ステーションからグリーンバイクの自転車を借り出す際にパスを利用し、1 ドルの解錠料金から 50% の割引を受けてください。これはトライシティーズで二輪車を利用する、もう一つの理由に過ぎません！

今すぐ TRIPLE-MET のバイク＆レールを試してみましょう！

5 英文の内容について、以下の問いに答えましょう。

Q1 What can be inferred about the new bicycle parking facility?
(A) Train tickets are available at the entrance.
(B) It is free of charge for any train users.
(C) Your bike won't get wet on rainy days.
(D) The gates can be opened with your smartphone.

Q2 What is true about the bicycle share program?
(A) You can use your Bike-and-Rail User Pass to borrow a bike.
(B) TRIPLE MET trains carry the bikes to your station.
(C) It comes with a Bike-and-Rail pass.
(D) The bikes are located next to each station.

解答と解説

Q1 解答（C）
新しい駐輪施設についてどんなことが推測できますか?
(A) 入り口で列車の切符が買える。
(B) 列車利用者なら誰でも無料で使える。
(C) 雨の日に自転車が濡れない。
(D) ゲートがスマホで開けられる。

解説 冒頭で新しい駐輪施設が完成したとあり、3〜4行目にNow you can safely park your bicycle in covered, secure parking areas ...と続いています。このcoveredは（屋根に覆われた）の意味。したがって、雨に濡れることがないと書かれている(C)が正解です。

Q2 解答（A）
自転車共有プログラムについて正しいのはどれですか?
(A) バイク&レールのユーザーパスで自転車を借りることができる。
(B) TRIPLE METの列車が利用駅まで自転車を運んでくる。
(C) バイク&レールのパスがついてくる。
(D) 自転車は各駅の隣にある。

解説 最終段落の1〜3行目に、your Bike-and-Rail User Pass also gives you priority access to the GreenBike public bicycle share programとあり、そのあとに、Use your pass when you check out a GreenBikeと書かれています。このyour passはyour Bike-and-Rail User Passを、a GreenBikeは借りられる自転車を指しているので、「ユーザーパスで借りられる」という(A)が正解です。

次のUnitも
頑張ろう！

🎧 27

READING

難易度 ●●○○○ 1　　約360語（ふつう）　　仕様書／説明・解説

1 あなたはMixiVimという調理器具の説明書を読んでいます。製品の機能を理解し、買うか買わないかを決めましょう。　[学習目標時間25分]

●まず、以下の英文を3分半を目標に読んでみましょう。次ページの「単語のヘルプ」も、必要に応じて参考にしてください。

Advanced Kitchen Tips: Making Soups with Your MixiVim All-in-One Food Processor

Tip #1: Making Nutritious Smoothies

There's nothing like a smoothie, iced drink or milkshake made with the patented MixiVim mixing and blending system. To make your delicious, nutritious smoothies even better, try these tips developed by our recipe development team with the help of top chefs. Remember, it matters how you load your ingredients. Start by pouring small amounts of liquid into the mixing container. Next, add softer fruits like bananas or orange slices. Finally, place ice or frozen fruits on top. This will enable your MixiVim blades to do their work most efficiently. For thicker, richer smoothies, use slightly less liquid. For thinner, more quenching smoothies, use slightly more liquid, and substitute whole milk with low-fat or nonfat milk. As with any recipe, spend time experimenting with ingredients like greens, berries and carrots. Half the fun is coming up with your own uniquely satisfying creations.

Tip #2: Heating Soups

You probably know about the MixiVim for its ability to produce delicious smoothies, iced drinks, milkshakes and purees. But the MixiVim All-in-One Food Processor is more than just a blender. One of the features that professional chefs like about MixiVim is its ability not only to make soups and sauces but to heat them for serving. This is because MixiVim features specially shaped blades and rotation speeds of up to 500 revolutions per second. When operating at top speed, the

MixiVim's blades not only thoroughly blend your soups, but they create friction energy that generates heat. If you blend cold tap water at top speed, it will boil in about eight minutes. Whether you are making a creamy celery mushroom soup or a clear broth, simply place the ingredients in the MixiVim, turn the speed dial to 10, its top setting, and blend for five to six minutes. The result will be a deliciously fresh soup, piping hot and ready to serve.

単語のヘルプ

他にもわからないものがあったら辞書で調べて書き足しておきましょう。

☐ nutritious 栄養価の高い ☐ patented 特許取得済みの

☐ recipe 調理法 ☐ matter 大事である

☐ load 乗せる ☐ ingredient （料理の）材料

☐ pour 注ぐ ☐ place 置く

☐ blade 刃 ☐ slightly わずかに

☐ quenching 喉の渇きをいやす ☐ substitute A with B AをBと代える

☐ whole milk 全乳 ☐ low-fat milk 低脂肪牛乳

☐ nonfat milk 無脂肪牛乳 ☐ as with 〜 〜と同様に

☐ experiment 試してみる ☐ greens 葉野菜

☐ come up 現れる ☐ puree ピューレ

☐ feature 特徴 ☐ revolution 回転

☐ thoroughly 完全に ☐ friction energy 摩擦エネルギー

☐ broth スープ ☐ piping hot （料理が）熱々の

TASK

2 読んだ英文を基に、この製品を買うか買わないかを選び、その理由を下線に英語で書いてみましょう（解答例は p. 162）。

☐ I'll buy this product.
☐ I don't think I'll buy this product.

_____

_____

_____

_____

_____

_____

_____

_____

_____

_____

☑ I'll buy this product.

I'm a mother of three small children. My days are extremely busy, so I am in great need of something like this product. I have three reasons to buy one. First, it sounds easy to use. Put the ingredients in the order and that's it! It's ideal for a person like me. Second, you can get nutritious drinks. It's very important to have something nourishing every day, especially for my children, but it's also difficult to try to cook everything yourself. The food processor makes it possible. Finally, it can serve soup hot. You don't need to heat it after blending. It's amazing. For these reasons, I'll definitely buy one.

日本語訳

3人の小さい子どもを持つ母親です。毎日がとても忙しいので、こうした製品はぜひほしいものです。購入の理由は3つあります。まず、使いやすそうだからです。順番に材料を入れれば、それで完了！ 私のような人には理想的です。次に、栄養のある飲み物をとれること。栄養価の高いものを毎日とることは、特に子どもたちにとってとても大事ですが、すべてを自分で料理をしようとするのは難しいことでもあります。このフードプロセッサーはそれを可能にしてくれます。最後に、スープを温かい状態で出せること。ブレンダーにかけたあとで温める必要がありません。すごいことです。こうした理由から、私は絶対に買おうと思っています。

☑ I don't think I'll buy this product.

The product seems good for some people, but not me. I'm the type of person who would rather eat fruit and vegetables as they are. Of course, I cut them up before eating but mixing and blending is too much. They might lose some of their nutrition. Also, serving food hot is great, but I enjoy time cooking and heating soup over a low flame the traditional way. By the way, how much is it? With these functions and the fact that it's popular among famous chefs, it is likely to be expensive. I would rather spend a little more for good qualify food like organic vegetables. That's how I enjoy my life.

日本語訳

この製品は一部の人たちにはいいのでしょうが、私には向きません。私は果物や野菜をそのまま食べたいほうです。もちろん、食べる前に切りますが、混ぜるのはやりすぎです。栄養が失われてしまうかもしれません。また、温かい料理を出すのはすばらしいことですが、私は時間をかけてスープをことことと温める昔ながらの方法が好きです。ところで、価格はどのぐらいなのでしょうか。こうした機能がついていて、有名なシェフから人気があるということは、高価なのでは。私だったら、有機野菜などの質のよい食材にもう少しお金をかけます。それが私の人生の楽しみ方です。

3 読み方のコツ

● 命令ではない命令形

動詞から始まる文のことを命令形と言いますが、手順を説明する場合には必ずしも命令しているわけではありません。ここでは、

try these tips ... (Tip #1の3行目)
Start by pouring ... (Tip #1の5行目)
add softer fruits ... (Tip #1の6行目)
place ice or frozen fruits ... (Tip #1の7行目)

をはじめ、多くの「命令文」が使われていますが、もちろん「〜しろ」ではなく、「〜します」という感覚でとらえるべき言い回しです。なお、

simply place the ingredients ... (Tip #2の下から4〜3行目)

のように、動詞の前に副詞が入る命令形もあります。

● 無生物主語

人ではなく、物事を主語とする用法です。

This will enable your MixiVim blades to ... (Tip #1の7〜8行目)

の This や、

Half the fun is coming up ... (Tip #1の下から2〜1行目)

の Half the fun がそれにあたります。

読んで理解する分には問題ないけれど、自分で書けるかどうかは疑問——もしそう感じているのであれば、無生物主語が出てきたときに、文脈での意味と使われている動詞をメモしておくと、のちのち役立ちます。

● 修飾語の追加

Unit 11で取り上げた後置修飾は、ここでも、

milkshake made with the patented MixiVim mixing and blending system (Tip #1の1〜2行目)
these tips developed by our recipe development team (Tip #1の3〜4行目)

で使われています。それぞれ下線部の名詞 (句) を made や developed 以下が説明しています。

それ以外に、

10, its top setting, (Tip #2の下から3行目)

の同格の用法にも注意が必要です。「its top setting (その最大設定値) である10」と、カンマだけで「〜である」を表しています。また、カンマさえない例も見かけます。うまく意味が通らないときは「同格かもしれない」と考えてみましょう。

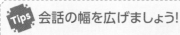

Tips 会話の幅を広げましょう!

手順を説明する際には、命令形に加えて、順番を表す語句を使うとわかりやすくなります。ゆで卵の作り方を例にとってみましょう (世の中には、さまざまな方法があるようなので、まったく違う作り方をされている方々も多いとは思いますが)。

1. 鍋に水を注ぎ、卵を入れる
2. 10分間、火にかける
3. 火からおろして、鍋にふたをし、5分間待つ
4. 冷水が入ったボウルに、卵を5分間ほど入れる

次のように、まず何の説明であるかを明確にし、そのあとで、順序立てて述べるといいでしょう。

In order to make hard-boiled eggs, follow these simple steps. First, pour tap water into a pot and put eggs in it. Second, heat the water 10 minutes. Next, turn off the heat, put a lid on the pot and leave it for five minutes. Finally, put the eggs into a bowl filled with iced water and leave them for five minutes. Now you're ready to peel them. (固ゆで卵を作るには、次の簡単な方法に従ってください。まず、鍋に水道水を注ぎ、そこに卵を入れます。2番目に、それを10分間火にかけます。次に、火からおろして、鍋にふたをし、そのまま5分間待ちます。最後に、冷水が入ったボウルに卵を5分間入れておきます。これで殻をむく用意ができました)

よりよく英文を理解するために音声を使って学びます。ポーズの箇所で、意味を考えながら、繰り返し□に出してみましょう。

 27

Advanced Kitchen Tips: / Making Soups with Your MixiVim All-in-One Food Processor //

Tip #1: / Making Nutritious Smoothies //

There's nothing like a smoothie, iced drink or milkshake / made with the patented MixiVim mixing and blending system. // To make your delicious, nutritious smoothies even better, / try these tips developed by our recipe development team / with the help of top chefs. // Remember, / it matters how you load your ingredients. // Start by pouring small amounts of liquid / into the mixing container. // Next, / add softer fruits like bananas or orange slices. // Finally, / place ice or frozen fruits on top. // This will enable your MixiVim blades / to do their work most efficiently. // For thicker, richer smoothies, / use slightly less liquid. // For thinner, more quenching smoothies, / use slightly more liquid, / and substitute whole milk with low-fat or nonfat milk. // As with any recipe, / spend time experimenting with ingredients / like greens, berries and carrots. // Half the fun is coming up / with your own uniquely satisfying creations. //

Tip #2: / Heating Soups //

You probably know about the MixiVim / for its ability to produce delicious smoothies, iced drinks, milkshakes and purees. // But the MixiVim All-in-One Food Processor is more than just a blender. // One of the features / that professional chefs like about MixiVim is its ability / not only to make soups and sauces but to heat them for serving. // This is because MixiVim features specially shaped blades / and rotation speeds of up to 500 revolutions per second. // When operating at top speed, / the MixiVim's blades not only thoroughly blend your soups, / but they create friction energy that generates heat. // If you blend cold tap water at top speed, / it will boil in about eight minutes. // Whether you are making a creamy celery mushroom soup or a clear broth, / simply place the ingredients in the MixiVim, / turn the speed dial to 10, / its top setting, / and blend for five to six minutes. // The result will be a deliciously fresh soup, / piping hot and ready to serve. //

　　　一歩進んだ料理の秘訣：MixiVim オールインワンフードプロセッサーで作るスープ
秘訣その1：栄養価の高いスムージーを作る
特許取得済みの MixiVim ミキシング・ブレンディングシステムで作ったスムージー、冷たい飲み物、ミルクセーキに勝るものはありません。あなたが日ごろ作っている、おいしくて栄養価の高いスムージーをより一層いいものにするために、当社の調理法開発チームが最高級シェフの力を借りて制作したこの秘訣を試してみてください。忘れていけないのは、材料の入れ方が大事だということ。まず、ミキサーの容器に液体を少々入れます。次に、スライスしたバナナやオレンジなど柔らかめの果物を加えます。最後に、氷または冷凍果物を一番上に乗せてください。こうすることで、MixiVim の刃が最も効率的に作動します。もっととろみがあって味が濃い目のスムージーにしたいときは、水分の量をやや減らします。さらっとして喉の渇きを癒す系のスムージーにしたい場合は、水分の量をやや増やし、全乳の代わりに低脂肪または無脂肪の牛乳を使用します。どんな調理法にも言えることですが、時間を見つけて葉野菜、ベリー、ニンジンなどの材料を試しに入れてみるといいでしょう。楽しみの半分は、あなた独自の満足いく創作から生まれます。
秘訣その2：スープを温める
おいしいスムージー、冷たい飲み物、ミルクセーキ、ピューレを作る性能があるとして MixiVim をご存じなのではないでしょうか。しかし MixiVim オールインワンフードプロセッサーは単なるブレンダーを超えています。MixiVim をプロのシェフが気に入っている特徴の一つは、スープやソースを作るだけでなく、それを温めて出せることです。これは MixiVim が特別な形の刃と毎秒最大500回転の回転速度を特徴としているからです。最高速度で操作すると、MixiVim の刃はスープを完全にブレンドするだけでなく、熱を発生させる摩擦エネルギーを生み出します。冷たい水道水を最高速度で混ぜると、約8分で沸騰するほどです。クリーミーなセロリマッシュルームスープを作るにしても澄んだスープを作るにしても、MixiVim に材料を入れ、スピードダイヤルを最大値の10に設定して、5〜6分間ブレンドするだけです。これで、おいしい新鮮なスープが、熱々ですぐに食卓に出せる状態でできあがります。

英文の内容について以下の問いに答えましょう。

Q1 Which is the right order to put ingredients into the blender?
(A) Liquid, softer fruits and frozen fruits
(B) Softer fruits liquid and frozen fruits
(C) Frozen fruits liquid and softer fruits
(D) Softer fruits, frozen fruits and liquid

Q2 How does the blender heat the food?
(A) There is a heater in the product.
(B) It uses the blade especially designed for heating.
(C) Friction caused by the blades generates heat.
(D) The pipes running inside warms the blender.

解答と解説

Q1 解答（A）
ブレンダーに材料を入れる適切な順番はどれですか？
(A) 液体、柔らかめの果物、冷凍果物
(B) 柔らかめの果物、液体、冷凍果物
(C) 冷凍果物、液体、柔らかめの果物
(D) 柔らかめの果物、冷凍果物、液体

解説 Tip #1の4～5行目で、it matters how you load your ingredients（材料の入れ方が大事である）とあり、Start by pouring ... liquid、Next, add softer fruits、Finally, place ice or frozen fruitsと続いているので正解は(A)です。

Q2 解答（C）
ブレンダーはどのようにして料理を温めるのですか？
(A) 製品の中に発熱器がある。
(B) 発熱用に特別に設計された刃を使う。
(C) 刃による摩擦が熱を発生させる。
(D) 内部にはりめぐらされた配管でブレンダーを温める。

解説 Tip #2の4～5行目で、its ability ... but to heat them for serving（料理を温めて出す性能）とあり、その仕組みとして7～9行目にthe MixiVim's blades ... create friction energy that generates heat（MixiVim の刃は熱を発生させる摩擦エネルギーを生む）と説明されているので正解は(C)です。

よく頑張りました！

オンライン口座を開くには

難易度 ●●● ・ 3 | 約320語（ふつう） | サービス利用開始／説明・解説

1 オンライン口座の開設手続きについて読み、利用者のタイプによってどの
口座が最も適切かを考えましょう。　　　　　[**学習目標時間25分**]

● まず、以下の英文を3分を目標に読んでみましょう。次ページの「単語のヘルプ」
も、必要に応じて参考にしてください。

When it's time to open a new bank account, make the most of your online options. If you are already familiar with a bank, check out its website to find out whether its online banking services are right for you. Most online banking services allow you to explore what they offer before you commit to opening a savings or checking account. Try this at several online banks to get a feel for what kinds of services and user interfaces you prefer.

For simple online banking, sending and receiving money electronically, and online shopping payments, an ordinary savings account is good enough. Savings accounts usually pay a small amount of interest on your account balance and offer access to debit and credit cards. Checking accounts usually don't pay interest, but they enable you to write paper checks or to order the bank to mail payments by check drawing on your account. This can be useful if you make frequent or numerous payments and want to avoid electronic fund transfer fees because banks usually do not charge checking account holders for these services. There are also hybrid or "interest checking" accounts, which offer some check-writing services and pay interest, although usually at lower rates than savings accounts. When you decide on a bank, look carefully at the account types and services they offer, and choose the account type that's right for you.

When you're ready to open your account, start by assembling the information you will need. If you are not yet a legal adult, you will need an adult parent or guardian to co-sign the account. Most banks require

the following information from you:
- Your full name and mailing address
- Your date of birth
- Your driver's license or other government-issued ID details
- Your social security or tax ID number

（　単語のヘルプ　）

他にもわからないものがあったら辞書で調べて書き足しておきましょう。

☐ bank account　銀行口座

☐ make the most of ～　～を最大限に活用する

☐ be familiar with ～　～をよく知っている　　☐ check out　調べる

☐ explore　（詳しく）調査する　　☐ commit to ～　～に取り組む

☐ savings account　普通預金口座　　☐ checking account　当座預金口座

☐ get a feel for ～　～の感触をつかむ

☐ user interface　ユーザーインターフェイス、パソコン画面の使い勝手

☐ electronically　電子的に、インターネットで

☐ interest　利子、利息　　☐ balance　残高

☐ access to ～　～を利用すること

☐ debit card　デビット（即時決済）カード

☐ enable A to do　A が～できるようにする

☐ paper check　小切手　　☐ check drawing　小切手の振り出し

☐ frequent　頻繁な　　☐ numerous　数多い

☐ transfer fee　振込手数料　　☐ charge　料金を請求する

☐ hybrid　混合の　　☐ rate　率

☐ assemble　集める　　☐ legal adult　法律上の成人

☐ guardian　保護者　　☐ co-sign　連署する

☐ social security number　社会保障番号

☐ tax ID number　納税者番号

TASK

2 お客さまA、Bの事情と希望を音声で聞いて、もっとも適切な口座を勧めましょう。以下の下線に英語で書き入れてください。不要な情報を排除することも必要です（解答例はpp. 172-173）。

🎧 **28**

Customer A　会社員

勧める口座の種類 _____

お客さまへの説明 _____

_____

_____

_____

Customer B　大学生

勧める口座の種類 _____

お客さまへの説明 _____

_____

_____

_____

Customer A a savings account, an interest checking account
If you would like to use checks for your transaction, an interest checking acount is good for you. It pays you interest, too. If checks are not necessary, a savings account will suit you.（お取引に小切手がお入り用であれば利子付き当座預金口座がいいでしょう。利息もお支払いいたします。小切手が不要でしたら、普通預金口座がよろしいかと思います）

[英文スクリプトと訳]
I'm working for a department store. It's been 10 years since I joined the company. I was just promoted to section manager last month. Of course, I do have a bank account for my salary, but I need a new one for my second job that will start next month. That's an import business dealing with wine. At the beginning, there will be only a small amount of money transferred into the account, but I hope it will grow big in the future. It would be nice if interest could be paid.（私はデパートで働いています。入社10年になります。先月課長に昇進したばかりです。もちろん給与振込み用の銀行口座は持っていますが、来月始める副業のために新規口座が必要なのです。ワインの輸入業務です。最初は口座に入金される額は少ないでしょうが、将来は大きく成長していってほしいと期待しています。利子の支払いがあればいいと思っています）

Customer B a savings account
A savings account would be good for you. But if you are a minor, you will need an adult guardian to co-sign the account. If you are not, it's not necessary.（普通預金口座がよろしいと思います。ただし、お客様が未成年の場合は、成人した保護者の方に連帯保証人になっていただく必要があります。未成年でなければ、それは不要です）

[英文スクリプトと訳]
I'm a university student majoring in business administration. This is my first year in college. I just started a part-time job at a cafe. I need a bank account to get paid, but I don't know anything about opening one. I heard there are two or three types of accounts. Please let me know which one would suit me and what information you need from me. I also want to have a credit card, if possible.（僕は経営学を専攻している大学生です。1年生です。カフェでアルバイトを始めたばかりです。給与を受け取るのに銀行口座が必要ですが、開設のしかたがまったくわかりません。口座には2〜3種類あるとのこと。僕に合っているのはどれなのか、僕について

どんな個人情報が必要なのかを教えてください。できれば、クレジットカードも持ちたいと思っています）

 英文を理解するには、こうした社会経験や一般知識もプラスになります。

3 読み方のコツ

● 段落とキーセンテンス

「各段落にはその内容をまとめているキーセンテンスがあり、ほとんどの場合、第一文がそれにあたる」というルールを聞いたことがあるかもしれませんが、それがすべてにあてはまるわけではありません。

このユニットの英文の構成は次のようになっています。

第1段落　概要
第2段落　具体的な説明
第3段落　手順の説明

第1段落の内容を発展させたのが第2段落ですが、そこでinterest checking accountが初めて登場するなど、やや変則的な構成です。また、第2段落のように、例示だけの段落も珍しくありません。締めの文として最後にWhen you decide on a bank, ... that's right for you.とありますが、これをキーセンテンスとすることはできません。

テクニックや一般論に頼らず、流れを追っていくことが大事です。

● 2つの複合名詞

a savings or checking account（第1段落5行目）
debit and credit cards（第2段落4～5行目）
an adult parent or guardian（第3段落3行目）
social security or tax ID number（最終行）
上記の語句に共通するのは、もともと2つの複合名詞だったものがつながったという点です。つまり、

a savings account or a checking account
a debit card and a credit card
an adult parent or an adult guardian
a social security number or a tax ID number
をそれぞれまとめて表現したもの。あわてて読んでいると、debitとcredit cardのように分けて理解してしまうこともありそうです。

なお、andでつなげた場合には、名詞が複数形になることにも注意しましょう（orならどちらか一方なので単数形）。the Upper and Lower Houses（上院と下院）、Kanagawa and Chiba prefectures（神奈川県と千葉県）のように、固有名詞についても同様です。

会話の幅を広げましょう!

銀行で使う基本用語をチェックしましょう。下線部に日本語に合った英語を入れてください。

1. I'll show you how to 引き出す cash at an ATM.
2. Insert your cash card here and put in your account number and 暗証番号.
3. The company will 振り込む your salary into your bank account on the 25th of each month.
4. This is the best way to 送金する to your country.
5. You should check how much the after-hour 手数料 is.

答え
1. withdraw（ATMで現金を引き出す方法を教えます）
   →名詞形 withdrawal を使うなら make a withdrawal。
2. PIN（ここにキャッシュカードを入れて、口座番号と暗証番号を入力します）
   → PINは personal indentification number の略。
3. deposit（会社は毎月25日にあなたの銀行口座に給料を振り込みます）
   →名詞として使うなら make a deposit。
4. transfer（これがあなたの国に送金するもっともよい方法です）
   →名詞として使うなら make a money transfer。
5. commission fee（営業時間外の手数料を確認したほうがいいですよ）
   →請求する場合は charge a commission。

Unit
13

よりよく英文を理解するために音声を使って学びます。ポーズの箇所で、意味を考えながら、繰り返し口に出してみましょう。

🎧 **29** ⋯⋯⋯⋯⋯⋯⋯⋯⋯⋯⋯⋯⋯⋯⋯⋯⋯⋯⋯⋯⋯◆

When it's time to open a new bank account, / make the most of your online options. // If you are already familiar with a bank, / check out its website to find out / whether its online banking services are right for you. // Most online banking services allow you to explore what they offer / before you commit to opening a savings or checking account. // Try this at several online banks / to get a feel for what kinds of services / and user interfaces you prefer. //

For simple online banking, / sending and receiving money electronically, and online shopping payments, / an ordinary savings account is good enough. // Savings accounts usually pay a small amount of interest on your account balance / and offer access to debit and credit cards. // Checking accounts usually don't pay interest, / but they enable you to write paper checks / or to order the bank to mail payments by check drawing on your account. // This can be useful / if you make frequent or numerous payments / and want to avoid electronic fund transfer fees / because banks usually do not charge checking account holders for these services. // There are also hybrid or "interest checking" accounts, / which offer some check-writing services and pay interest, / although usually at lower rates than savings accounts. // When you decide on a bank, / look carefully at the account types and services they offer, / and choose the account type that's right for you. //

When you're ready to open your account, / start by assembling the information you will need. // If you are not yet a legal adult, / you will need an adult parent or guardian / to co-sign the account. // Most banks require the following information from you: //

- Your full name and mailing address //
- Your date of birth //
- Your driver's license / or other government-issued ID details //
- Your social security or tax ID number //

日本語訳

新たに銀行口座を開設するときには、オンライン口座を最大限に活用しましょう。知っている銀行がある場合、その銀行のウェブサイトでネット銀行サービスがあなたに合っているかどうかを調べます。ほとんどのネット銀行サービスでは、普通口座や当座預金口座の開設を決める前に、サービス内容を調べることができます。これをいくつかのネット銀行で行い、どんな種類のサービスや利用者画面が自分の好みか、感触をつかんでみましょう。

　簡単なネット銀行取引、電子的な送金・入金、オンラインショッピングの支払いであれば、通常の普通預金口座で十分です。普通預金口座は、残高に対して支払われる利子は通常少額で、また、デビットカードやクレジットカードの引き落とし口座に指定できます。当座預金は大抵の場合、利子は発生しませんが、小切手を切ることや、自分の口座に小切手を振り出すことで銀行に対してメール決済を請求することができます。これは、頻繁にまたは数多くの支払いを行なっていて、電子送金手数料を回避したい場合に便利です。というのも、銀行は通常、当座預金保持者にはこうしたサービスの手数料を課していないからです。また、ハイブリッド型、いわゆる、「利子付き当座預金」口座もあり、ある程度の小切手振り出しサービスを提供し、普通口座に比べれば率は低いことが通常であるものの、利子が支払われます。取引銀行を決める際は、提供されている口座の種類とサービス内容を注意深く調べて、ご自分に合った種類の口座を選びましょう。

　口座開設の準備ができたら、まず必要となる情報を集めることから始めます。法的に成人に達していない場合は、口座の連帯保証人となる親または保護者が必要です。ほとんどの銀行で求められる情報は以下の通りです。

- ・ フルネームと住所
- ・ 誕生日
- ・ 運転免許証などの政府が発行する身分証明書の詳細内容
- ・ 社会保障番号または納税者番号

Q1 Which bank account does NOT usually incur interest?
    (A) A savings account
    (B) A checking account
    (C) An interest checking account
    (D) None of the above

Q2 Which information is NOT usually asked for when opening a bank account?
    (A) Your date of birth
    (B) Your address
    (C) Your identification card
    (D) Your income certificate

解答と解説

Q1 解答 (B)
通常、利子が発生しない銀行口座はどれですか?
(A) 普通預金口座
(B) 当座預金口座
(C) 利子付き当座預金口座
(D) 上記のどれでもない

解説 それぞれの銀行口座のサービスに関しては、第2段落で説明されています。5行目に Checking accounts usually don't pay interest とあるので正解は (B) です。(A) については3行目に Savings accounts usually pay a small amount of interest と、(C) については下から5行目に There are also hybrid or "interest checking" accounts, which ... pay interest と書かれています。

Q2 解答 (D)
銀行口座を開設する際に通常求められない情報はどれですか?
(A) 誕生日
(B) 住所
(C) 身分証明書
(D) 収入証明書

解説 口座開設の際に求められる情報については最終段落の箇条書き部分に書かれています。(A) は Your date of birth に、(B) は Your ... mailing address にあり、(C) は Your driver's license or other government-issued ID details のこと。Your tax ID number は書かれていますが、収入を証明するものではないので、正解は (D) です。

Unit
13

銀行関連の用語、
この際きちんと覚えておきましょう。

30-31　　　　　　　　　　　　　　　**READING**

1 トレーニングジムで、マシーンの使い方について説明書きを読みます。そのあとで、手順を説明してみましょう。　[**学習目標時間30分**]

●まず、以下の英文を3分を目標に読んでみましょう。次ページの「単語のヘルプ」も、必要に応じて参考にしてください。

Using Gym Equipment at Fittique Gyms

When you use a piece of gym equipment for the first time, be sure to familiarize yourself with it before you start. Improper use can injure your muscles, joints and bones.

Each Fittique Gym fitness machine is located in its own Fitness Station. When you're ready to use a machine, follow the floor markings and signs. These will provide easy-to-understand instructions on how to adjust and use the machine safely and effectively. Floor markings show you where to line up and wait if the machine is in use and where to enter and exit the Fitness Station. Signs posted at each exercise station include handy QR codes you can use to download text and 30-second video instructions.

Many beginners prefer to start with the cable machine because it is relatively easy to use and provides the versatility of exercising many basic muscle groups at one station. The instruction panel will show you how to adjust the apparatus to your height, your leg length and your arm length where necessary. Everyone's body is different, so be sure to make the adjustments to ensure a fit that's just right for you.

If you aren't familiar with your strength capacity, start with the lightest available weight setting. A few easy repetitions will warm up your muscles and joints, while familiarizing you with the motions you'll be making before you add significant resistance. Before adding weights, consider making additional adjustments to the machine so you feel comfortable through the full range of the exercise motion. Start your exercises with a weight that you can comfortably lift, push or pull for two or three repetitions without tiring. There's plenty of time to challenge yourself later, when you're thoroughly familiar with the equipment.

When you are finished with your repetitions, wipe any perspiration from the grips or pads of the machine, and if the gym is crowded, move promptly on.

〔 単語のヘルプ 〕

他にもわからないものがあったら辞書で調べて書き足しておきましょう。

☐ gym equipment　ジム機材

☐ familiarize oneself with 〜　〜をよく知る

☐ improper　不適切な　　　　　　☐ injure　傷つける、痛める

☐ instructions　取扱説明　　　　　☐ line up　列に並ぶ

☐ in use　使用中で　　　　　　　☐ post　掲示する

☐ handy　便利な　　　　　　　　☐ relatively　比較的

☐ versatility　多用途性　　　　　☐ apparatus　器具

☐ fit　ぴったりと合う感覚　　　　☐ strength capacity　強度容量

☐ available　（最上級とともに）利用可能なかぎりの

☐ repetition　繰り返し、反復（運動）　☐ resistance　負荷

☐ range　範囲　　　　　　　　　☐ thoroughly　完全に

☐ wipe　拭く　　　　　　　　　☐ perspiration　汗

☐ pad　クッション部分　　　　　☐ move on　立ち退く

☐ promptly　すぐに

TASK

2　下のイラストを使って（もとの英文はできるだけ見ずに）、ジムでマシーンを利用する際の手順を英語で説明しましょう（解答例は p. 184）。

a

_____

_____

_____

b

_____

_____

_____

c

_____

_____

_____

d

_____

_____

_____

e

_____

_____

_____

f

_____

_____

_____

g

_____

_____

_____

h

_____

_____

_____

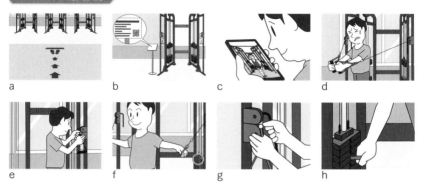

a. Follow the markings on the floor to and out of the exercising machine area. When all the machines are being used, wait where designated.（エクササイズマシーンエリアの出入りには床にある印に従って進んでください。すべてのマシーンが使用中の場合は、指定された場所で待っていてください）

b. Each exercise machine has a sign showing how to use it.（エクササイズマシーンにはそれぞれ使い方を示す表示があります）

c. The sign comes with a QR code to download an instruction video.（表示には使い方ビデオをダウンロードできるQRコードがついています）

d. Cable machines are popular because they are easy to use for beginners.（ケーブルマシーンは初心者にとって使いやすいので人気があります）

e. Read the instruction panel on each machine to adjust it to your height and the lengths of your arms and legs.（各マシーンについている使い方のパネルを読んで、ご自分の身長、手足の長さに合わせて調整してください）

f. Start exercises with light weights. Make repetitions two or three times as warm-ups.（エクササイズは軽いウエイトから始めてください。ウォームアップとして、2〜3回動きを繰り返します）

g. Again, make sure the machine fits you perfectly. Adjust it if necessary.（再度、マシーンの設定がご自分に合っているかを確認します。必要であれば調整してください）

h. You can add weights and see if it's not too challenging.（ウエイトを増やして、負荷が強過ぎないかどうか確認してください）

答え合わせのあとに、音声でも聞いてみましょう。

🎧 **30** ....◆

3 読み方のコツ

● 省略

where necessary (第3段落5行目)

は、where it is necessary の it is が省略されたものです。when necessary (必要なときには) という言い方もよく使われます。また、

while familiarizing (第4段落3行目)

Before adding (第4段落4行目)

も、それぞれ while you are familiarizing、Before you add のこと。このようにわかりきっている主語と be 動詞を省略する (必要なときは動詞を ing 形にする) ことがよくあります。when や after にも同様の用法があります。

　省略される主語は本来、主節の主語と同じでなければならないというルールがあるものの、上記の while familiarizing (主節の主語は A few easy repetitions) のように、その限りではない例も多く見かけるようになりました。

● 最上級の修飾

the lightest available weight setting (第4段落1～2行目)

は最上級を available で修飾する用法。the lightest weight setting (最も軽いウエイトの設定) に available をつけて「その器具でできる範囲で」の意味を付け加えています。似たような表現に、possible を使うものがあります。いくつか例を挙げましょう。

the best possible solution (できる限り最善の解決方法)

the worst possible scenario (考えうる最悪の事態)

the funniest possible joke (考えられる中で最もおもしろいジョーク)

the shortest possible time (できるだけ最短の時間)

なお、the best solution possible などのように、possible をうしろにつける用法もあります。

最近よく耳にするcardioはもともと「心臓の」の意味で、cardio exerciseを短くした言い方。aerobics同様、「有酸素運動」のことです。その目的は脂肪燃焼(to burn fat)またはカロリー燃焼(to burn calories)です。「筋トレ(muscle exercise)」もブームですね。インストラクターの口からは「腹筋(abdominal muscle, abs)」「太ももの裏の筋肉であるハムストリングス(hamstrings)」「上腕二頭筋(biceps)」「上腕三頭筋(triceps)」といった筋肉の名称が頻繁に聞かれます。より日常的な運動としては、「腕立て伏せ(push-ups)」「腹筋運動(sit-ups, crunches)」「懸垂(chin-ups)」があります。いずれも動詞はdoです。そして、最後には「深呼吸をする(to take a deep breath)」ことで、その日のエクササイズを終えます。

よりよく英文を理解するために音声を使って学びます。ポーズの箇所で、意味を考えながら、繰り返し口に出してみましょう。

 31 ⋯⋯⋯⋯⋯⋯⋯⋯⋯⋯⋯⋯⋯⋯⋯⋯⋯⋯⋯⋯⋯⋯⋯⋯⋯⋯⋯⋯⋯⋯⋯⋯⋯⋯

When you use a piece of gym equipment for the first time, / be sure to familiarize yourself with it before you start. // Improper use can injure your muscles, joints and bones. //

Each Fittique Gym fitness machine is located in its own Fitness Station. // When you're ready to use a machine, / follow the floor markings and signs. // These will provide easy-to-understand instructions / on how to adjust and use the machine safely and effectively. // Floor markings show you where to line up and wait / if the machine is in use / and where to enter and exit the Fitness Station. // Signs posted at each exercise station include handy QR codes you can use / to download text and 30-second video instructions. //

Many beginners prefer to start with the cable machine / because it is relatively easy to use / and provides the versatility of exercising many basic muscle groups at one station. // The instruction panel will show you how to adjust the apparatus / to your height, your leg length and your arm length where necessary. // Everyone's body is different, / so be sure to make the adjustments to ensure a fit that's just right for you. //

If you aren't familiar with your strength capacity, / start with the lightest available weight setting. // A few easy repetitions will warm up your muscles and joints, / while familiarizing you with the motions you'll be making / before you add significant resistance. // Before adding weights, consider making additional adjustments to the machine / so you feel comfortable through the full range of the exercise motion. // Start your exercises with a weight / that you can comfortably lift, push or pull for two or three repetitions without tiring. // There's plenty of time to challenge yourself later, / when you're thoroughly familiar with the equipment. //

When you are finished with your repetitions, / wipe any perspiration

Unit
14

from the grips or pads of the machine, / and if the gym is crowded, move promptly on. //

┌─────────────┐
│ **日本語訳** │
└─────────────┘

フィティック・ジムでジム機材を使う

ジム機材を初めて使う場合には、始める前に必ずその機材のことをよく知るようにしましょう。不適切に使用すると、筋肉、関節、骨を傷めることがあります。

　フィティック・ジムのフィットネスマシーンは、それぞれのフィットネスステーションに設置されています。マシーンを使う準備ができたら、床に書かれた印や指示に従ってください。ここには、マシーンを安全かつ効果的に調整および使用する方法についてわかりやすい説明があります。床の印は、そのマシーンが使用中の場合にはどこで並んで待つか、また、フィットネスステーションにはどこから出入りするのかが示されています。それぞれのエクササイズステーションに掲示されている指示には、文字情報と30秒の動画説明をダウンロードするために使える便利なQRコードも付いています。

　初めてご利用される方の多くが、比較的使いやすく、また、一箇所で多くの基本筋肉群のエクササイズができるという汎用性があるという理由で、ケーブルマシーンから始めることを選択されます。使用方法パネルには、身長、足の長さ、腕の長さに合わせ、必要に応じて器具を調整する方法が書かれています。体型は一人ひとり異なりますので、必ず、ご自分にきちんと合った状態に調整してください。

　ご自分の強度容量がおわかりにならない場合は、重量設定値の最も軽いところから始めましょう。簡単な反復練習を何度か行うと筋肉や関節のウォーミングアップになり、同時に、多くの負荷を加える前に、これから行なっていく運動に慣れることにつながります。ウエイトを追加する前に、全可動域の動きを通して心地よく感じるように、マシーンを再度調整することを検討してみてください。持ち上げたり、押したり、引いたりするのを2～3回繰り返しても疲れず、楽にできるウエイトからエクササイズを始めましょう。自分を追い込むのは、その機材にすっかり慣れてから、後ほどいくらでも時間があります。

　エクササイズを何度かし終えたら、マシーンの取っ手やクッション部分から汗を拭き取り、ジムが混んでいれば、速やかに移動しましょう。

英文の内容について以下の問いに答えましょう。

Q1 In the gym, what would you use your smartphone for?
(A) Showing the waiting time before entering the gym
(B) Learning how to use each machine
(C) Adjusting the exercise machines quickly
(D) Giving instructions to the staff members

Q2 According to the explanation, what should a beginner do before adding weight to a machine?
(A) Wipe the sweat off the machine
(B) Familiarize yourself with the gym
(C) Do some exercise with lower resistance settings
(D) Decide when to start the exercise

解答と解説

Q1 解答（B）
そのジムでスマートフォンを使うとしたら、それは何のためですか？
(A) ジムに入るまでの待ち時間を表示する
(B) それぞれのマシーンの使い方を知る
(C) エクササイズマシーンを手早く調整する
(D) スタッフに指示を与える

解説 第2段落の最後にSigns posted at each exercise station include handy QR codes you can use to download text and 30-second video instructions. とあることから、文字情報と動画説明をダウンロードできるとわかります。このジムでスマートフォンを使うとすればそのためなので、正解は (B) です。

Q2 解答（C）
この説明によれば、マシーンにウエイトを追加する前に初心者がすべきことは何ですか？
(A) マシーンから汗を拭き取る
(B) ジムについてよく知る
(C) 低めの負荷設定でエクササイズを行う
(D) いつエクササイズを開始するかを決める

解説 第4段落冒頭に、If you aren't familiar with your strength capacity, start with the lightest available weight setting. とあります。マシーンに慣れていなければ（つまり初心者は）、最軽量のウエイトから始めるべきということなので、正解は (C) です。

難易度 ●●● ○○ 3 ｜ 約300語（ふつう） ｜ 物件紹介／案内

> **1** あなたはヒルハースト大学に通う学生です。現在、引っ越しを考えており、賃貸物件のリストを見ています。以下を読んで内容を把握しましょう。
>
> [**学習目標時間40分**]

● まず、以下の英文を3分を目標に読んでみましょう。次ページの「単語のヘルプ」も、必要に応じて参考にしてください。

Student Housing Rental Listings

Hillhurst neighborhood:

ROOM RENTAL in spacious four-bedroom house. This is a large bedroom on the ground floor near a quiet backyard. The renter will have their own bathroom and can use the back door of the house as an exclusive private entrance and exit. The location is ideal for students as it is located a 10-minute walk from the Hillhurst University campus East Gate. Cooking is not allowed in the room, and the kitchen will be shared with the owners. Contact Tom and Cindy at cmnbrns7089@rgaderlink.com for information.

HOUSEMATES SOUGHT: We are a group of four Hillhurst College drama and literature majors looking for two housemates to share a rental home. The location is on Graphin Avenue near the Third Street intersection. We have reserved a lease and can guarantee a room to the right housemates. Please contact Sarah at sstenney9917@hhcoll.edu for more information on the house, our group of housemates and the house rules we are in the process of setting up. We plan to meet the landlord at the house on Saturday the 12th, which will be an opportunity for approved prospective housemates to see the property.

APARTMENT SHARE: I have a large private room available for sublet in a shared three-bedroom apartment in the Silver Valley district. We are friendly, quiet and considerate NON-SMOKING women graduate students who seek similar. Rental includes access to a shared washer and dryer in the hallway. Room rent is $825 per month, with first and last months' rent due on signing the sublet agreement. The property owners live on the premises and will participate in the candidate approval decision. Please contact subletsv4321@rmail.com. Tell us about yourself, your work, your habits and how long you expect to live in the apartment. References are a plus.

(単語のヘルプ)

他にもわからないものがあったら辞書で調べて書き足しておきましょう。

- [ ] spacious　広い
- [ ] exclusive　専用の
- [ ] ～ major　～専攻の学生
- [ ] reserve　（権利を）保有する
- [ ] lease　賃借権
- [ ] guarantee　保証する
- [ ] in the process of ～　～の過程において
- [ ] landlord　家主
- [ ] prospective　将来の
- [ ] property　物件
- [ ] sublet　転貸
- [ ] considerate　思いやりのある
- [ ] access to ～　～を利用すること
- [ ] hallway　廊下
- [ ] due　支払うべき
- [ ] agreement　契約
- [ ] premises　敷地
- [ ] candidate　候補者
- [ ] reference　紹介状
- [ ] plus　さらなる利点

TASK

2 入居希望者の面接で、それぞれの住居に入居を許可されるような自己紹介の文を書いてみましょう（解答例は p. 194）。

a. a house a 10-minute walk from the Hillhurst University campus East Gate

_____

_____

_____

_____

_____

b. a house on Graphin Avenue near the Third Street intersection

Unit
15

_____

_____

_____

_____

_____

c. an apartment in the Silver Valley district

_____

_____

_____

_____

_____

a. a house a 10-minute walk from the Hillhurst University campus East Gate

Hi. My name is _____. I believe I'm a good candidate for the prospective housemate because I'm cooperative and easy to talk to. Also, as I work part-time at a cafe from 7 in the morning, five days a week, it would be nice to have my exclusive exit so that I won't disturb my housemates. I've been looking for a place like this.（こんにちは、私の名前は_____です。私は協力的で話しやすい性格なので、同居人としてふさわしいと思っています。それに、週5日、朝の7時からカフェでアルバイトをしているので、自分専用の出口があれば、みなさんを起こさないですみ、好都合です。こんな家を探していました）

b. a house on Graphin Avenue near the Third Street intersection

Hello. I'm _____. Nice to meet you. I'm a junior at Hillhurst and very friendly and sociable. I used to live in a dorm for the first- and second-year students, and I didn't have any problems. My major is art. And I believe I have a lot to share with all of you. It would be my great pleasure if I could start my new life there.（こんにちは、_____です。はじめまして。私はヒルハーストの3年生で、性格は友好的かつ社交的です。1〜2年生用の寮に2年間住んでいて、何も問題はありませんでした。専攻は美術です。それにみなさんと共有できることがたくさんあると思っています。ここで新しい生活を始められればとってもうれしく思います）

c. an apartment in the Silver Valley district

Hello. My name is _____. Thank you for having me. I'm a senior at collge and thinking of continuing my studies at grad school. If I'm selected, I can learn a lot from you. I'm a bookworm and I spend most of my time reading and writing —— which means I'm a very quiet person. Of course, I don't smoke.（こんにちは、_____と申します。お呼びいただきありがとうございました。私は大学4年生で、大学院で研究を続けようと思っています。もし選ばれれば、みなさんからいろいろなことが学べます。私は本が大好きで、ほとんどの時間、読んだり書いたりしています。ですから、かなり物静かなほうです。もちろん、タバコは吸いません）

③ 読み方のコツ

● 前置詞

前置詞は日本語にないので要注意。また、数多ある英単語の中でほんの数十語しかない前置詞は一つひとつが多くの意味を持つため、文脈に合うように正確に理解する必要があります。ひとつの訳語をすべての場合に当てはめようとしてはいけません。

たとえば、第1段落下から2行目の

Contact Tom and Cindy at ...

の at は電話番号やメールアドレスなど連絡先の前につける前置詞です。a professor at ABC University (ABC 大学の教授) のように所属を表す場合も at です。「in は広いところを、at は狭いところを指す」という「ルール」とは異なりますね。

また、第3段落5行目の

with first and last months' rent due on signing ...

の with は with A B の形で「A を B の状態にして」と付帯状況を表します。ここでは A にあたるのが first and last months' rent、B にあたるのが due です。また、この on は on ...ing (…するときに) の形で使われています。したがって、「署名するときに最初と最後の月の家賃を支払い期限の状態として」、つまり、「署名した時点で最初と最後の月の家賃を払うという条件で」の意味になります。

● 後置修飾

Unit 11 で、後置修飾には「名詞+分詞 (句)」以外に「名詞+形容詞 (句)」の形もあると説明しましたが、その例が、第3段落1行目の

a large private room available for sublet ...

で、available 以降が room を後ろから修飾しています。seven habits common with rich people (富裕層に共通する7つの習慣) のように common にも、名詞のあとに続く用法があります。

● 単数形と複数形

日本語では単数と複数の違いをあまりはっきりさせないため、つい見落としがちなポイントです。当然のことですが、複数形にするということは抽象名詞ではなく、数えられる名詞として使われているとわかります。

第3段落最終行の reference がその良い例。「参考」「言及」など数えられない名詞としてとらえると意味が通じません。ここでは references と複数形になっているので、「1枚、2枚…と数えられる推薦状」を指しているとわかります。ですから、この文は「推薦状があればより好ましい」という意味になります。

会話の幅を広げましょう!

日本語では、「私は社交的です」のように自分を売り込むことはまだまだ少ないようですが、英語では臆することなく、I'm sociable. などと言ったりします。ここでは、「自分のいい性格を表す」語句をいくつか挙げておきます。ほとんど知っている語句でしょうが、自分にとってどれが使えるかを考える機会にしてください（まずは、自分にあてはまるものにチェックを入れましょう）。

☐ active（活発な）
☐ ambitious（意欲的な）
☐ brave（勇敢な）
☐ calm（落ち着いた）
☐ candid（率直な）
☐ caring（心優しい）
☐ cheerful（元気のいい）
☐ cooperative（協力的な）
☐ creative（創造的な）
☐ dedicated（献身的な）
☐ devoted（献身的な）
☐ energetic（元気な）
☐ enthusiastic（熱意のある）
☐ fun to be with
　（一緒にいて楽しい）

☐ generous（寛容な）
☐ good listener, a
　（人の話をよく聞く人）
☐ hardworking（勤勉な）
☐ honest（正直な）
☐ knowledgeable（物知りの）
☐ neat（きれい好きな）
☐ organized（きちんとした）
☐ polite（礼儀正しい）
☐ reliable（頼りになる）
☐ responsible（責任感のある）
☐ self-confident（自信のある）
☐ sociable（社交的な）
☐ thoughtful（思いやりのある）
☐ witty（機知に富んだ）

> **4** よりよく英文を理解するために音声を使って学びます。ポーズの箇所で、
> 意味を考えながら、繰り返し口に出してみましょう。

🎧 **32**

Student Housing Rental Listings //

Hillhurst neighborhood: //

ROOM RENTAL in spacious four-bedroom house. // This is a large bedroom on the ground floor near a quiet backyard. // The renter will have their own bathroom / and can use the back door of the house / as an exclusive private entrance and exit. // The location is ideal for students / as it is located a 10-minute walk from the Hillhurst University campus East Gate. // Cooking is not allowed in the room, / and the kitchen will be shared with the owners. // Contact Tom and Cindy at / cmnbrns7089@rgaderlink.com for information. //

HOUSEMATES SOUGHT: // We are a group of four Hillhurst College drama and literature majors / looking for two housemates to share a rental home. // The location is on Graphin Avenue / near the Third Street intersection. // We have reserved a lease and can guarantee a room to the right housemates. // Please contact Sarah at / sstenney9917@hhcoll.edu for more information on the house, / our group of housemates / and the house rules we are in the process of setting up. // We plan to meet the landlord at the house on Saturday the 12th, / which will be an opportunity for approved prospective housemates / to see the property. //

APARTMENT SHARE: // I have a large private room available for sublet / in a shared three-bedroom apartment / in the Silver Valley district. // We are friendly, quiet and considerate NON-SMOKING women graduate students / who seek similar. // Rental includes access to a shared washer and dryer in the hallway. // Room rent is $825 per month, / with first and last months' rent / due on signing the sublet agreement. // The property owners live on the premises / and will participate in the candidate approval decision. // Please contact

Unit **15**

subletsv4321@rmail.com. // Tell us about yourself, your work, your habits / and how long you expect to live in the apartment. // References are a plus. //

学生向け賃貸物件リスト

ヒルハースト地区：寝室が4部屋ある広々とした一軒家。静かな裏庭の近くにある一階の大きな寝室です。貸主専用のバスルームがあり、家の裏口を専用の出入り口として使うことができます。ヒルハースト大学東門から徒歩10分と学生には理想的な立地です。部屋での調理は禁止されており、キッチンはオーナーと共用になります。詳細については、トムとシンディー（cmnbrns7089@rgaderlink.com）までご連絡ください。

求む同居人：私たちはヒルハースト大学で演劇と文学を専攻している4人のグループで、貸し家を共有する2人の同居人を探しています。場所はグラフィン通りの3番街との交差点の近くです。私たちはすでに賃借権を保有しているので、同居人としてふさわしい方には部屋を保証することができます。家屋、同居人グループ、および現在設定中の住居ルールの詳細については、sstenney9917@hhcoll.edu のサラにお問い合わせください。12日の土曜日に大家さんと現地で会う予定になっていて、入居を許可された方に物件を見ていただく機会となります。

アパート共有：シルバーバレー地区の寝室が3室ある共有アパートに、大きな個室を転貸用に用意しています。私たちは親しみやすく、物静かで、思いやりがあり、非喫煙者である女子大学院生で、似たような方を求めています。賃貸には、廊下にある共用の洗濯機と乾燥機の使用が含まれます。部屋代は月額825ドルで、最初と最後の月の分は転貸契約締結時の支払いとなります。物件所有者は同敷地内にお住まいで、入居候補者の承認決定に参加します。subletsv4321@rmail.com までご連絡ください。あなた自身のこと、仕事、習慣、アパート居住予定期間を教えてください。紹介状があればより有利です。

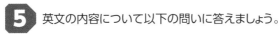

5 英文の内容について以下の問いに答えましょう。

Q1 Which room could you enter without being noticed?
  (A) The one that has easy access to the university campus
  (B) The one near the intersection of Graphin Avenue and the Third Street
  (C) The one located in the Silver Valley district
  (D) None of the above

Q2 How much would a successful candidate for the third apartment need to pay when she signs the agreement?
  (A) $825
  (B) $1,650
  (C) $2,475
  (D) $3,300

Unit
15

解答と解説

Q1 解答(A)
人に気づかれずに入れる可能性がある部屋はどれですか?
(A) 大学のキャンパスに行きやすい物件
(B) グラフィン通りと3番街の交差点に近い物件
(C) シルバーバレー地区にある物件
(D) 上記のどれでもない

解説 第1段落2〜4行目の物件紹介に、The renter ... can use the back door of the house as an exclusive private entrance and exit.と専用の出入り口があると書かれているので、この部屋には他の人に気づかれずに入れる可能性があります。したがって、正解は(A)です。

Q2 解答(B)
3軒目のアパートに入居を許された人が契約時に払わなければならない金額はいくらですか?
(A) 825ドル   (B) 1,650ドル
(C) 2,475ドル   (D) 3,300ドル

解説 第3段落5〜6行目の中ほどにあるRoom rent is $825 per month, with first and last months' rent due on signing the sublet agreement.の on signingは「署名時に」の意味。契約にサインしたときに払うのは最初と最後の月、つまり、2カ月分の家賃なので825ドルを倍にした(B)が正解です。

Reading を鍛える！

Chapter 4
読んだ情報を相手に伝える　上級編

最後のChapterでは、ネイティブが日常的に目にしているフォームや小説の抜粋などにチャレンジします。最初はTASKに答えられるように、最終的には細かい部分まで理解できるよう、音声も使って丁寧に読み込んでみましょう。

33-34 **READING**

難易度 ●●● ● ● 3 | 約500語（長い）| 免責同意書／説明・解説

1 次の英文を読んで内容を理解し、読み手がどうすることを求められている
かを把握しましょう。 [学習目標時間30分]

●まず、以下の英文を5分を目標に読んでみましょう。次ページの「単語のヘルプ」
も、必要に応じて参考にしてください。

Joline Caverns State Park: Underground Adventure Walk and Obelisk Observation Deck
RELEASE OF LIABILITY FORM

Note: Your signed and dated copy of this release of liability is required with your admission ticket when you enter the Joline Caverns State Park Site. This is an agreement that limits our liability. Please read it carefully before signing. Release forms are available online, by mail, and at the park vehicle and pedestrian entrances.

Visitor Rules & Responsibilities

- When you enter the park grounds (including parking lots and driveways), you do so at your own risk. Admittance is not allowed without a signed copy of this release form.
- Persons under the age of 18 must be accompanied by a legally responsible adult (parent or guardian).
- All visitors must be free of medical conditions or disabilities that prevent walking unaided on uneven and slippery ground, and on unstable surfaces such as suspension bridges.
- NO SMOKING: Smoking is not permitted anywhere in the park at any time.
- Additional CAUTION signs are posted at cave entrances, inside caves, at suspension bridges and other areas to warn of hazards. Read all signs and follow instructions carefully. STAY SAFE!
- Use restrooms before leaving the park Entrance Area. No restrooms

are available in the cave and walkway areas.

- Keep our park clean. No trash cans are available beyond the park Entrance Area, and littering is prohibited in the park. If you pack it into the park, pack it out!
- If you see coyotes, bears or other large wildlife, remain in the protected path areas. Leave them alone, and they will leave you alone. Never attempt to feed or interact with wildlife, including birds and fish.
- Violations of these and other posted park rules may result in fines or other penalties. Rescues made necessary by negligence, reckless behavior or other rule violations could also result in fines.

Please provide the following information for each visitor:

Full name (print): _____

Planned activities (check all that apply): ☐ Sightseeing, ☐ Hiking, ☐ Rock climbing, ☐ Cave walking, ☐ Wading, ☐ Picnicking

Unit **16**

I agree that my use of the State Park facilities and premises is undertaken entirely at my own risk. I assume all risk of injury, illness, damage or loss to me or my property that might occur during my visit. I freely consent to any rescue action, first aid and/or other medical treatment as deemed necessary by Park Management Personnel in the event that any injury, accident or illness should occur during my visit. I agree to assume financial responsibility for all such medical treatment and/or rescue action. I agree to release Park Management from responsibility for any damages arising from alleged negligence. I acknowledge that I have carefully read and understood the above information, and that I agree to these terms.

Signature of visitor* _____

date /   / _____

(*or accompanying adult if under 18)

単語のヘルプ

他にもわからないものがあったら辞書で調べて書き足しておきましょう。

- ☐ obelisk 方尖塔
- ☐ observation deck 展望台
- ☐ release 免除
- ☐ liability 法的責任
- ☐ admission ticket 入場券
- ☐ agreement 同意
- ☐ pedestrian 歩行者
- ☐ at one's own risk 自分の責任において
- ☐ admittance 入場
- ☐ accompany 同伴する
- ☐ guardian 保護者
- ☐ free of 〜 〜がなくて
- ☐ medical condition 身体疾患、健康状態
- ☐ disability 障害
- ☐ unaided 人の手を借りない
- ☐ uneven 平らではない、起伏のある
- ☐ slippery 滑りやすい
- ☐ unstable 不安定な
- ☐ suspension bridge 吊り橋
- ☐ post 掲示する
- ☐ cave 洞窟
- ☐ warn of 〜 〜を警告する
- ☐ hazard 危険
- ☐ walkway 歩道
- ☐ trash can ゴミ箱
- ☐ littering （ゴミの）ポイ捨て
- ☐ pack it out （ゴミなどを）持ち帰る
- ☐ coyote コヨーテ
- ☐ wildlife 野生動物
- ☐ feed 餌付けする
- ☐ interact with 〜 〜と関わりあう
- ☐ violation 違反（行為）
- ☐ fine 罰金
- ☐ negligence 不注意、過失
- ☐ reckless 無謀な
- ☐ wade （水の中を）歩く
- ☐ premises 敷地
- ☐ undertake 取り組む、行う
- ☐ assume （責任を）負う
- ☐ property 所有物
- ☐ freely 無制限に
- ☐ consent to 〜 〜に同意する
- ☐ medical treatment 治療
- ☐ deem 思う
- ☐ arise 生じる
- ☐ alleged 〜 〜と疑われる、推定の〜
- ☐ acknowledge 認める
- ☐ term 条項

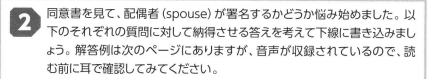

2 同意書を見て、配偶者 (spouse) が署名するかどうか悩み始めました。以下のそれぞれの質問に対して納得させる答えを考えて下線に書き込みましょう。解答例は次のページにありますが、音声が収録されているので、読む前に耳で確認してみてください。

Spouse: It says, "When you enter park grounds, you do so at your own risk." This means it's very dangerous in there, right?

You: _____

_____

Spouse: How about the next clause, "Persons under the age of 18 must be accompanied by a legally responsible adult"? Sam is always running around and it's hard to always keep an eye on him.

You: _____

_____

Spouse: Oh, there's no restroom available in the park. I wonder if Sam can do without one. He always says, "I want to go pee" at the last minute.

You: _____

_____

Unit **16**

Spouse: One more thing about Sam. When the animals show up, do you think he can leave them alone? He might start shouting or screaming with excitement.

You: _____

_____

Spouse: By the way, how's that leg you twisted? Is it back to normal? The form says you should be free of injuries and that rescues would cost money.

You: _____

_____

Spouse: OK. You convinced me. Let's sign the agreement.

音声でも聞いてみましょう。

🎧 33 ....

Spouse: It says, "When you enter park grounds, you do so at your own risk." This means it's very dangerous in there, right?

You: You know, it's a wildlife park. You can't say it's 100 percent safe. I think we'll have more fun than worry.

Spouse: How about the next clause, "Persons under the age of 18 must be accompanied by a legally responsible adult"? Sam is always running around and it's hard to always keep an eye on him.

You: Don't worry. I will tell him to stick with us. He's already five, you know. And I'll take hold of his hand all the time.

Spouse: Oh, there's no restroom available in the park. I wonder if Sam can do without one. He always says, "I want to go pee" at the last minute.

You: Let's not have anything to drink before entering the park. You and me included. Also, we'll just let him have fun when in the park, and he'll be fine.

Spouse: One more thing about Sam. When the animals show up, do you think he can leave them alone? He might start shouting or screaming with excitement.

You: Again, let's tell him about the rule. He's old enough to understand. We still have three weeks to go, and it's enough time for the idea to sink in. And if he does end up shouting and the animal seems to be coming toward us, I'll do everything to protect him, and of course, you.

Spouse: By the way, how's that leg you twisted? Is it back to normal? The form says you should be free of injuries and that rescues would cost money.

You: Never mind. It'll be perfect by the time we go there.

Spouse: OK. You convinced me. Let's sign the agreement.

日本語訳

配偶者：「公園の敷地内に入る際は、自己責任でお願いします」と書いてあるね。つまり、その中はとても危険だということでしょ？

あなた：まあ、野生動物公園だから。100％安全とは言えないよ。心配より楽しいことのほうが多いと思うけど。

配偶者：次の「18歳未満の方には法的に責任のある成人の同伴が義務付けられている」という条項は？　サムはいつも走り回っていて、ひと時も目を離さないというのは難

しい。

あなた：大丈夫。いつも一緒にいるように僕／私が言うから。もう5歳だよ。それに、僕／
　　　　私がずっと手をつないでいるし。

配偶者：あ、公園の中にはトイレがない。サムは（トイレ）なしで大丈夫かな。いつもぎりぎ
　　　　りになって「おしっこしたい」って言うから。

あなた：公園に入る前は水分を取らないようにしよう。僕／私たちも。それに、公園にいる
　　　　ときは楽しいことをさせておけば、大丈夫だよ。

配偶者：サムのことでもうひとつ。動物が現れたら、ちょっかいを出さないでおけると思う？
　　　　興奮して大声を出したり叫んだりするはずだから。

あなた：その規則についても言っておこう。もうわかる歳だ。まだ3週間あるし、そういう考
　　　　えを理解するには十分時間があるよ。それに、サムが叫んで、動物がこっちに来る
　　　　ようなら、サムと、もちろん君／あなたを守るために何でもするし。

配偶者：ところで、くじいた足はどう？　元に戻った？　この用紙にはけがをしていないこと
　　　　が条件で、救助されたらお金がかかるって書いてあるから。

あなた：心配ないよ。行くときにはすっかり治っているよ。

配偶者：わかった。それで納得。同意書に署名しましょう。

答え合わせをした後に、音声を聞きましょう。

 33

Unit
16

❸ 読み方のコツ

● 語句同士の組み合わせ①

語句と語句の自然な組み合わせ、いわゆるコロケーションには、「動詞＋名詞」「形容詞＋名詞」「前置詞＋名詞」「名詞＋動詞」「名詞＋前置詞」「形容詞＋前置詞」などさまざまな形があります。また、「なぜそう使われるのか」と問われても、「それが自然だから」としか言いようがないという「特徴」を持っています。

英文を読んだり聞いたりするときには常に意識し、一つひとつ自分のものにしていきましょう。

ここでは、

assume financial responsibility

の assume と responsibility がコロケーションの例です。この assume を「推測する」の意味でとらえると responsibility とつながりません。

この at your own risk で risk には前置詞 at がつくこと、free of ... で free に of が続いて「…がない」の意味になるのも、「そういうふうに言うのが普通だから」というのが理由です。

● 語句同士の組み合わせ②

日本語にしづらい語句にも注目しましょう。その代表格と言えるのが、

alleged negligence

の alleged です。この単語だけを辞書で引くと、「申し立てられた」と出てきますが、それでは negligence とのつながりがはっきりしません。alleged は「～をしただろうと疑われた／言われた状態」を表し、

alleged tax evasion（脱税疑惑）

alleged murderer（殺人容疑者）

のように使われます。

また、Visitor Rules & Responsibilities の第7項目にある

If you pack it into the park, pack it out!

も、そのままでは何のことだかわかりません。もともとは、

If you pack it, pack it out!（持って入ったものは持ち帰りましょう）

という山などでの合言葉で、ゴミの持ち帰りをうながす表現です。ここでは多少の変更を加えて使われています。

このように、うまく意味がとれないときには、前後の単語も一緒に調べてみるといいでしょう。

● 語句同士の組み合わせ③

文法面で忘れがちな項目にも要注意です。Visitor Rules & Responsibilities の第8項目の

Leave them alone, and they will leave you alone.

の「命令形＋and ...」は「〜すれば…するでしょう」の意味です。

Never attempt to feed or interact with ...

では interact の前に attempt to が省略されています。このように、「AもBもない」は not/never A and B ではなく、not/never A or B で表現することも忘れないようにしましょう。

Unit
16

Tips 会話の幅を広げましょう！

危険を知らせるもっとも一般的な標識は

Caution

です。本文に出てきた野生動物との接近を禁止する場所には、

No Feeding (Animals)

No Feeding or Touching Animals

といった標識が立っているでしょう。同様に No ...ing の形で

No Trespassing（立ち入り禁止）

No Entry（進入禁止）

No Pedestrians（歩行者立ち入り禁止）

などがさまざまな行為を禁止します。また、

Beware of ...（…に注意）

の of のあとには、crocodiles、snakes、bears などの動物の種類を続けて、その出没に対する警戒を促します。

Road/Trail Closed Ahead（この先、道路／自然道通行止め）

Slippery Walkway（滑りやすい歩道に注意）

Wet Paint（ペンキ塗りたて）

のように、状態だけを示したものもあります。

よりよく英文を理解するために音声を使って学びます。ポーズの箇所で、意味を考えながら、繰り返し口に出してみましょう。

 34

Joline Caverns State Park: / Underground Adventure Walk and Obelisk Observation Deck /
RELEASE OF LIABILITY FORM //

Note: / Your signed and dated copy of this release of liability is required with your admission ticket / when you enter the Joline Caverns State Park Site. // This is an agreement that limits our liability. // Please read it carefully before signing. // Release forms are available / online, by mail, and at the park vehicle and pedestrian entrances. //

Visitor Rules & Responsibilities //

- When you enter the park grounds / (including parking lots and driveways), / you do so at your own risk. // Admittance is not allowed / without a signed copy of this release form. //
- Persons under the age of 18 / must be accompanied by a legally responsible adult / (parent or guardian). //
- All visitors must be free of medical conditions or disabilities / that prevent walking unaided on uneven and slippery ground, / and on unstable surfaces such as suspension bridges. //
- NO SMOKING: / Smoking is not permitted anywhere in the park at any time. //
- Additional CAUTION signs are posted / at cave entrances, inside caves, at suspension bridges and other areas / to warn of hazards. // Read all signs and follow instructions carefully. // STAY SAFE! //
- Use restrooms before leaving the park Entrance Area. // No restrooms are available in the cave and walkway areas. //
- Keep our park clean. // No trash cans are available beyond the park Entrance Area, / and littering is prohibited in the park. // If you pack it into the park, / pack it out! //
- If you see coyotes, bears or other large wildlife, / remain in the protected path areas. // Leave them alone, and they will leave you

alone. // Never attempt to feed or interact with wildlife, / including birds and fish. //

- Violations of these and other posted park rules / may result in fines or other penalties. // Rescues made necessary by negligence, reckless behavior or other rule violations / could also result in fines. //

Please provide the following information for each visitor: //

Full name / (print) /: _____

Planned activities / (check all that apply): / ☐ Sightseeing, / ☐ Hiking, / ☐ Rock climbing, / ☐ Cave walking, / ☐ Wading, / ☐ Picnicking //

I agree that / my use of the State Park facilities and premises is undertaken / entirely at my own risk. // I assume all risk of injury, illness, damage or loss to me or my property / that might occur during my visit. // I freely consent to any rescue action, first aid and/or other medical treatment / as deemed necessary by Park Management Personnel / in the event that any injury, accident or illness should occur during my visit. // I agree to assume financial responsibility / for all such medical treatment and/or rescue action. // I agree to release Park Management from responsibility / for any damages arising from alleged negligence. // I acknowledge that I have carefully read and understood the above information, / and that I agree to these terms. //

Signature of visitor* / _____

date ___ / ___ / ___

(*or accompanying adult if under 18) //

Unit
16

211

ジョリーン・ケイバーンズ州立公園：地下探検歩道と方尖塔展望デッキ
賠償責任免責同意書

注意：ジョリーン・ケイバーンズ州立公園敷地内に立ち入る際は、入場券とともに署名および日付記入済みのこの免責同意書が求められます。これは、当方の法的責任を限定する同意書です。署名する前に、注意深く読んでください。免責同意書の用紙はインターネット上、郵送、そして、公園の車両歩行者入り口で入手できます。

入場者向け規則および入場者が負う責任

- 公園の敷地内（駐車場、園内道路を含む）に入る際は、自己責任でお願いします。署名済みのこの免責同意書がなければ、入場は認められません。
- 18歳未満の方には法的に責任のある成人（親または保護者）の同伴が義務付けられています。
- 入園者は全員、起伏があったり滑りやすかったり、地面や吊り橋のような足元が不安定だったりする場所を介助なしでは歩けないような病症や障害がないものとします。
- 禁煙：喫煙はいかなる時も公園の全域で禁止されています。
- さらなる警告標識が、洞窟の入り口、洞窟の内部、吊り橋などの場所に掲示され、危険を警告しています。すべての標識を注意深く読んで指示に従ってください。常に安全な状態でいてください！
- 公園の入り口区域を出る前にお手洗いをすませておいてください。洞窟や歩道区域にトイレはありません。
- 公園は常にきれいな状態にしておいてください。公園の入り口区域より先にはゴミ箱がなく、園内はゴミのポイ捨てが禁止されています。公園内でゴミが出たら、お持ち帰りください！
- コヨーテ、熊などの大型野生動物を見たら、遊歩道の保護区域内にとどまってください。放っておけば、向こうもみなさんを放っておきます。鳥や魚を含む野生動物に餌をやったり、触れ合ったりしようとは決してしないでください。
- 上記、およびこれ以外に掲示されている規則に違反すると、罰金などの罰が課せられることがあります。過失、無謀な行為などの規則違反によって必要となった救助行為に対しても罰金を求められる可能性があります。

入場者一人ひとりについて、以下の情報を提供してください。

フルネーム（ブロック体で記入）：

計画している行動（当てはまるものすべてにチェックマークを入れてください）：　□観光、□ハイキング、□岩登り、□洞窟散策、□川歩き、□ピクニック

私は、州立公園の施設および敷地の利用については全面的に自己責任において行うことを同意します。滞在中に起こるであろう私または私の所有物に対する、けが、病気、損害、または、紛失といったすべてのリスクを私が負います。滞在中に負傷、事故または病気が発生した際、公園管理者が必要とみなした救助行為、応急処置などの医療手当てについてはいかなるものも無条件で受け入れます。私は、そのようなすべての医療処置および／または救助活動に対する金銭的責任を負うことに同意します。私は、過失の疑いから生じたいかなる損害についても、公園管理局の責任を問わないことに同意します。私は、上記の情報を注意深く読み、理解し、これらの条件に同意したことを認めます。

利用者*の署名／_____

　　　　　　（日付）　　/　　/　　　（＊あるいは18歳未満の場合は同行する成人）

5 英文の内容について以下の問いに答えましょう。

Q1 What is this agreement mainly for?
   (A) Ensuring that all visitors will remain safe.
   (B) Releasing the park management from legal responsibility.
   (C) Protecting wildlife animals such as coyotes and bears.
   (D) Drawing attention to warning signs posted in the park.

Q2 What might happen if you disregarded the rules?
   (A) You might be ousted from the park.
   (B) You might be fined.
   (C) You might be taken to the police.
   (D) You might be forced to sign the agreement.

解答と解説

Q1 解答（B）
この同意書の主な目的は何ですか?
(A) 訪問者全員の安全を確実にすること。
(B) 公園管理局の責任を免除すること。
(C) コヨーテや熊などの野生動物を保護すること。
(D) 公園内に掲示された危険を知らせる標識に注意を向けること。

解説 選択肢のすべてが合っているように見えますが、問われているのは同意書の主な目的です。タイトルには、RELEASE OF LIABILITY FORMとあり、また、第1段落3行目にThis is an agreement that limits our liability.とあることから、この同意書の第一の目的は公園側の責任を免除するためのものだとわかります。したがって、正解は(B)です。

Q2 解答（B）
規則を無視したらどんなことが起こる可能性がありますか?
(A) 公園から追い出される。
(R) 罰金を科せられる。
(C) 警察に連行される。
(D) 強制的に同意書に署名させられる。

解説 Visitor Rules & Responsibilitiesの第9項目にViolations of these and other posted park rules may result in fines or other penalties.とあります。violations of ... rulesを設問ではdisregard the rulesと言い換えています。result in finesのfineが「罰金を科す」という意味の動詞で使われている(B)が正解です。

長めの英文に
挑戦しましょう！

35

READING

| 難易度 ●●●●● 5 | 約550語（長い） | 社会問題／ドキュメンタリー |

1 次の英文を読んで、何が問題なのかを明らかにし、さらに、その解決策を考えてみましょう。　　　　　[学習目標時間50分]

●まず、以下の英文を5分半を目標に読んでみましょう。次ページの「単語のヘルプ」も、必要に応じて参考にしてください。

Social trend researchers, media pundits and politicians are fond of describing U.S. woes as "epidemic." In recent years, Americans have been diagnosed with "epidemics" of obesity, opiate drug abuse, gun crime and even credit card debt. Adding one more ill to the list, a recent mental health study says that they are now in the midst of a national epidemic of loneliness.

The latest research from the Langston University Graduate School of Public Health Science includes survey research indicating that almost half of American adults, 48 percent, report feelings of loneliness severe enough to seriously reduce their quality of life. The percentage is higher among single adults, averaging 55 percent, and tends to be higher among those who say they do most of their social interaction online.

It wasn't supposed to be this way. Two decades ago, the combination of email and increasingly useful mobile phones, and the subsequent explosion in the popularity of social networking apps, seemed to promise the elimination of loneliness. In our new world of "connectedness," anyone could communicate with anyone else, anytime, anywhere. No more isolation. And yet, feelings of isolation and loneliness seem to be going from bad to worse, especially among youths who stay connected by video and text at all hours of the day and night. The conclusion seems to be that online connectedness cannot adequately replace fulfilling social interactions.

Professor Luciana Arkon, who led the Langston University study, calls this phenomenon "the dilution of social meaning." In the study, an extensive compilation of existing and new survey results and original mental health data, Arkon notes that "Shifting social interaction from face-to-face settings to online chat venues has increased the volume of social interaction without adding meaningful content." She argues that sending someone a quick text message, often while engaged in another activity, is easy and convenient. But it takes very little commitment. Compare that to making a date, committing an hour of your time, deciding on a cafe and then physically going there to meet the person you want to talk to. "Effort and commitment make a conversation more meaningful and more effective at preventing loneliness," she writes. The internet has made communication effortless by eliminating the need for effort or commitment.

People do, of course, express emotions online. But the study notes that the emotions expressed online tend toward feelings of anger, agitation and exasperation —— much like driving a car in traffic does. "We are depriving our younger generation of healthy face-to-face interactions that develop their social skills," Arkon says. "Earlier generations did this on the school playground, in clubs, through sports competition and through unstructured outdoor play. This has, by and large, been replaced by video games featuring various levels of simulated violence without real consequences."

It's clear that this could have devastating effects if these youth grow up to be adults who are not equipped to form meaningful relationships. Arkon suggests a nationwide effort to educate young people on how to make friends and how to discover their own purpose and future as members of an "in-person" society.

単語のヘルプ

他にもわからないものがあったら辞書で調べて書き足しておきましょう。

- ☐ pundit　評論家
- ☐ epidemic　伝染病
- ☐ be diagnosed with 〜　〜だと診断される
- ☐ obesity　肥満
- ☐ opiate drug abuse　アヘン薬物乱用
- ☐ in the midst of 〜　〜の真っただ中に
- ☐ report A (to be) B　AがBであると報告する
- ☐ average　平均すると〜となる
- ☐ social interaction　社会的交流
- ☐ subsequent　続く
- ☐ explosion　爆発
- ☐ app　アプリ
- ☐ elimination　排除
- ☐ isolation　孤立
- ☐ and yet　しかし
- ☐ go from bad to worse　悪化の一途をたどる
- ☐ at all hours　いつでも
- ☐ adequately　十分に
- ☐ replace　取って代わる
- ☐ fulfilling　充実した
- ☐ phenomenon　現象
- ☐ dilution　希薄化
- ☐ social meaning　社会的意義
- ☐ extensive　広範囲の
- ☐ compilation　収集
- ☐ existing　現存の
- ☐ face-to-face　対面の
- ☐ venue　場
- ☐ (be) engaged in 〜　〜に取り組む
- ☐ commitment　深い関与

Unit
17

- [ ] make a date 人と会う約束をする
- [ ] physically 実際に
- [ ] prevent 防ぐ
- [ ] effortless 楽な
- [ ] agitation あおり
- [ ] exasperation 憤慨
- [ ] in traffic 渋滞に巻き込まれて
- [ ] deprive A of B A から B を奪う
- [ ] sports competition スポーツ競技
- [ ] unstructured 枠が決まっていない
- [ ] by and large 概して
- [ ] feature ～ ～を特徴とする
- [ ] simulated 擬似的な
- [ ] consequences 結果
- [ ] devastating 壊滅的な
- [ ] be equipped to ～ ～する能力を備えている
- [ ] in-person 面と向かっての

TASK

2 読んだ英文から問題点を表している部分（複数箇所ある段落もあり）を抽出し、その意図を日本語で書き出してください。その後、他の人に問題提起をする形で、120語程度の英語で要点をまとめてみましょう（解答例はpp. 220-221）。

問題点を表している部分

第1段落

意図

第2段落

意図

第3段落

意図

第4段落

意図

第5段落

意図

第6段落

意図

まとめ

ポイント：意図は、英文を訳すのではなく、その本質のみを抽出します。該当する和訳と照らし合わせてみましょう。

第1段落

they are now in the midst of a national epidemic of loneliness

意図 全国的に孤独が蔓延している

第2段落

almost half of American adults, 48 percent, report feelings of loneliness severe enough to seriously reduce their quality of life

意図 孤独が原因で生活の質がかなり低下している

第3段落

feelings of isolation and loneliness seem to be going from bad to worse

意図 孤独や孤立がより深刻な問題になっている

第4段落

the dilution of social meaning

意図 人と人とのつながりが薄くなっている

Shifting social interaction from face-to-face settings to online chat venues has increased the volume of social interaction without adding meaningful content.

意図 ネット上での交流は表面的である

it takes very little commitment

意図 まったく深入りしない

The internet has made communication effortless by eliminating the need for effort or commitment.

意図 ネットでは楽してコミュニケーションができてしまう

第5段落

the emotions expressed online tend toward feelings of anger, agitation and exasperation

意図 ネットでの感情表現は否定的になりがちである

We are depriving our younger generation of healthy face-to-face interactions that develop their social skills.

意図 若い世代は人との付き合い方を学ぶ機会がない

第6段落

It's clear that this could have devastating effects if these youth grow up to be adults who are not equipped to form meaningful relationships.

意図 人間関係を築けないまま大人になるのは悲惨なことだ

まとめ

ポイント：相手の注意を引いてから本題に入るといいでしょう。

What do you think is one of the newest and the most talked-about diseases in the U.S.? Obesity? Drug abuse? No, it's loneliness. But here a question might come up: Why do people feel lonely in this internet era, when they can connect anyone regardless of time and place? It's because the connection is superficial and cannot replace real face-to-face interaction. Exchanging text messages and movies online is so easy that they don't need to put any energy into it. And the emotions they tend to show on the net is almost always negative. It's just not real social interaction. We need to do something about it, especially for the younger generation, who are growing up without learning what the meaningful relationships are.

Unit
17

日本語訳

アメリカで最も話題になっている最新の病気の一つは何だか知っていますか？　肥満？　麻薬乱用？　いいえ、それは孤独です。しかしここでひとつ疑問がわきます。いつでもどこでも誰とでも連絡が取りあえるこのインターネットの時代に、なぜ人々は孤独を感じるのでしょうか。それは、そうしたつながりが表面的で実際の対面での関わりの代わりにはならないからです。ネット上での携帯メールや動画の交換は簡単すぎて、労力をかける必要がありません。また、ネット上で表す感情はほぼ否定的なものです。それは実際の社会的な関わり合いとは異なります。こうしたことに対して私たちは行動を起こさなければならず、それは特に、意義のある人間関係とは何かを学ぶことなく大人になっていく若い世代に対して言えることです。

3 読み方のコツ

● and がつなぐもの①

A and B なら and がつないでいるのは A と B だと容易にわかりますが、第3段落の1〜4行目の、

Two decades ago, the combination of email <u>and</u> increasingly useful mobile phones, <u>and</u> the subsequent explosion in the popularity of social networking apps, seemed to promise the elimination of loneliness.

のように and が複数個、それも同じ主語の中に見つけた場合には、一瞬どれとどれをつないでいるか悩みます。ここでは、最初の and は、

the combination of A and B

のつながりで、email が A、increasingly useful mobile phones が B にあたります。また、2つ目の and は、

A and B seemed

の関係で、the combination ... phones が A、the subsequent explosion ... apps が B にあたります。なお、読みやすくするため、この and の前にはカンマがつけられています。前者では email と phones の、後者では combination と explosion のつながりであることが見えれば、頭も整理されますね。

● and がつなぐもの②

以前のユニットでも取り上げた並列は、I like baseball, soccer and basketball. のように、特にその順番に意味はありませんでしたが、第4段落下から6〜4行目の

Compare that to making a date, committing an hour of your time, deciding on a cafe and then physically going there to meet the person you want to talk to.

では、making a date（会う約束を取り付ける）から physically going there to meet ...（実際に会いに行く）まで、発生する順番に並んでいます。ここに並んでいる4つの要素（making ...、committing ...、deciding ...、going）を、それぞれ独立したつながりのない行動として捉えてしまうと、書き手の意図を正確には理解することができません。

● 日本語になりにくい commitment

第4段落下から6行目の commitment を辞書で引くと、「約束、献身、傾倒」などの訳があてられていますが、

it takes very little commitment

にあてはめても、「（他のことをしながら）手早くメールを送ることは、ほとんど約束／献身／傾倒を要さない」と、わかったようなわからないような日本語にしかなりません。

　最近はcommitやcommitmentを「コミットする」「コミットメントする」のようにカタカナで使われることもあるようですが、動詞commitの核となる意味「深く関わる」「一生懸命行う」から、その場に合った解釈をするといいでしょう。ここでは「ほとんど一生懸命にやっていない」から、かなりの意訳ですが、「心ここに在らず」としてみました。

Tips 会話の幅を広げましょう！

本文に出てきたexasperationの形容詞形はexasperated（憤慨した）。annoyedやvexedの同義語です。ただ、否定的な形容詞ばかり覚えても気分が暗くなってしまうので、ここでは肯定的な形容詞をいくつか挙げておきましょう。
- [ ] elated（大喜びの）
- [ ] exalted（喜びでいっぱいの）
- [ ] jubilant（大喜びの）
- [ ] ecstatic（熱狂した）
- [ ] enthusiastic（熱中した）
- [ ] exhilarated（浮き浮きした）
- [ ] uplifted（気持ちが高揚した）
- [ ] triumphant（意気揚々とした）
- [ ] relieved（ほっとした）
- [ ] motivated（やる気が湧いた）
- [ ] grateful（ありがたく思う）

　be動詞やfeelとともに、自分のことを話すときにぜひ使ってみてください。前向きな気持ちになれるはずです。

よりよく英文を理解するために音声を使って学びます。ポーズの箇所で、意味を考えながら、繰り返し口に出してみましょう。

35 ....◆

Social trend researchers, media pundits and politicians / are fond of describing U.S. woes as "epidemic." // In recent years, / Americans have been diagnosed with "epidemics" / of obesity, opiate drug abuse, gun crime and even credit card debt. // Adding one more ill to the list, / a recent mental health study says that / they are now in the midst of a national epidemic of loneliness. //

The latest research from the Langston University Graduate School of Public Health Science / includes survey research / indicating that almost half of American adults, 48 percent, / report feelings of loneliness / severe enough to seriously reduce their quality of life. // The percentage is higher among single adults, / averaging 55 percent, / and tends to be higher among those / who say they do most of their social interaction online. //

It wasn't supposed to be this way. // Two decades ago, / the combination of email and increasingly useful mobile phones, / and the subsequent explosion in the popularity of social networking apps, / seemed to promise the elimination of loneliness. // In our new world of "connectedness," / anyone could communicate with anyone else, anytime, anywhere. // No more isolation. // And yet, / feelings of isolation and loneliness / seem to be going from bad to worse, / especially among youths / who stay connected by video and text at all hours of the day and night. // The conclusion seems to be that / online connectedness cannot adequately replace fulfilling social interactions. //

Professor Luciana Arkon, / who led the Langston University study, / calls this phenomenon "the dilution of social meaning." // In the study, / an extensive compilation of existing and new survey results and original mental health data, / Arkon notes that / "Shifting social interaction from face-to-face settings to online chat venues / has increased the volume of social interaction without adding meaningful content." // She argues that / sending someone a quick text message, / often while engaged in another activity, / is easy and convenient. // But it takes very little commitment. // Compare that to making a date, / committing an hour of your time, / deciding on a cafe and then physically going there to meet the person you want to talk to. // "Effort and commitment make a conversation / more meaningful and more effective at preventing loneliness," / she writes. // The internet has made communication effortless / by eliminating the need for effort or commitment. //

People do, of course, express emotions online. // But the study notes that / the emotions expressed online tend toward feelings of anger, agitation and exasperation / —— much like driving a car in traffic does. // "We are depriving our younger generation of healthy face-to-face interactions / that develop their social skills," / Arkon says. // "Earlier generations did this / on the school playground, in clubs, through sports competition and through unstructured outdoor play. // This has, by and large, been replaced by video games / featuring various levels of simulated violence without real consequences." //

Unit
17

It's clear that / this could have devastating effects / if these youth grow up to be adults / who are not equipped to form meaningful relationships. // Arkon suggests a nationwide effort to educate young people / on how to make friends and how to discover their own purpose and future / as members of an "in-person" society. //

| 日本語訳 |

社会動向の研究者、メディアに登場する評論家、そして政治家は、アメリカの苦悩を「伝染病」と表現するのを好む。ここ数年、アメリカ人は肥満、アヘン薬物乱用、銃犯罪、さらにはクレジットカードによる借金といった「伝染病」にかかっていると診断されている。その一覧にもうひとつの疾病を加えると、最近の精神衛生の研究によれば、彼らは今、孤独の全国的な流行の真っただ中にいるという。

ラングストン大学公衆衛生科学大学院の最新の研究には、アメリカの成人のほぼ半数（48%）が、生活の質を著しく低下させるほどの深刻な孤独を感じているという報告がある。この割合は、独身の成人ほど高く、平均すると55%であり、ほとんどの社会的交流をオンラインで行っていると回答した層で高まる傾向にある。

こんなはずではなかった。20年前、電子メールと利便性がますます高まっていた携帯電話の組み合わせ、さらに、その後のソーシャルネットワーキングアプリの爆発的人気が、孤独感の排除を約束したように見えた。「つながっている状態」という私たちの新しい世界では、誰もがいつでもどこでも誰とでもコミュニケーションをとることができているはずだった。孤立はもはや過去のもの。それにもかかわらず、孤立感や孤独感は、特に昼夜を問わず動画や文字でつながっている若者の間で、悪化の一途をたどっているようだ。オンライン上で「つながっている状態」は、充実した社会的交流の十分な代用とはなりえないというのが結論のようである。

このラングストン大学による研究を指導したルチアナ・アルコン教授は、こうした現象を「社会的意義の希薄化」と呼ぶ。既存および新規の調査結果と精神衛生に関する元のデータを広範にまとめたこの研究で、アルコン教授は「社会的交流を対面での状況からオンラインチャットの場に移行したことで、社会的交流の量は増えたが、意味のある内容は追加されなかったということだ」と述べている。教授は、誰かにさっとメールを送るのは、しばしば他の活動に従事している間に行われるが、簡単で便利なことだと論じる。しかし、ほとんど心ここに在らずである。それと、人と会う約束をして、自分の時間を1時間費やし、どのカフェに行くかを決め、話したい相手に会うために実際にそこに行くことを比べてみてほしい。「努力と深い関与が会話をより意味のあるものにし、孤独を防ぐ効果を高める」と教授は書いている。インターネットは、努力や深い関与の必要性を排除することにより、コミュニケーションを楽にしたのである。

もちろん、人々はオンライン上でも感情を表現する。しかし、オンライン上で表現された感情は、怒り、あおり、憤りといった感情に向かう傾向があり、それはまるで渋滞の中で運転しているときのようだと、この研究は指摘している。「私たちは若い世代から、彼らの社交術を発達させる健全な対面交流の場を奪っている」とアルコン教授は言う。「それ以前の世代は学校の運動場やクラブ活動で、また、スポーツ競技や誰もが参加できる野外遊びでこれを行なっていた。こうしたことが概して、現実的な結果を伴わない、様々な度合いの模擬暴力を特徴とするテレビゲームに取って代わられた」。

こうした若者たちが、有意義な関係を築く能力が備わっていない大人に成長したら、このことが壊滅的な影響を及ぼす可能性があることは明らかだ。アルコン教授は、「対面」社会の一員として、どのようにして友だちを作り、どのようにして自分自身の目的と未来を見つけるかについて、若者たちを教育する全国的な取り組みの実施を提案している。

5 英文の内容について以下の問いに答えましょう。

Q1 Which is NOT listed as "epidemics" in the U.S. society?
(A) Drug abuse　　　　(B) Obesity
(C) Connectedness　　(D) Loneliness

Q2 What was expected by the growing technology of the internet?
(A) There would be a fewer people suffering from lonliness.
(B) People of all ages would send messages around the clock.
(C) The crime rate would decrease drastically.
(D) Mobile phones would become more and more useful.

解答と解説

Q1 解答（C）
アメリカ社会の「伝染病」として挙げられていないものはどれですか?
(A) 薬物乱用　　　　(B) 肥満
(C) つながり　　　　(D) 孤独

解説 第1段落3〜4行目で "epidemics" of obesity, opiate drug abuse, gun crime and even credit card debt と「伝染病」の具体例を挙げています。また最終行で、a national epidemic of loneliness と付け加えています。この of はどちらも「〜という」の意味。ここに含まれていない (C) が正解です。

Q2 解答（A）
インターネット技術の成長によって期待されていたことは何ですか?
(A) 孤独を感じる人が少なくなる。
(B) すべての年齢の人たちが四六時中メールを送信する。
(C) 犯罪発生率が劇的に減少する。
(D) 携帯電話が一段と便利になる。

解説 第3段落冒頭にある It wasn't supposed to be this way.（そういうようになるはずではなかった）がポイント。そのあとで、the combination of email and increasingly useful mobile phones ... seemed to promise the elimination of loneliness（メールと携帯電話の利便性が高まることで孤独感の排除が約束されたと思われた）と、また、6〜7行目で And yet, feelings of isolation and loneliness seem to be going from bad to worse（しかし、孤立感や孤独感は悪化の一途をたどっているようだ）と言っていることから、期待されていたことは (A) だとわかります。

36-37

READING

難易度 ●●● ○ ○ 3　　約420語（やや長い）　　自己啓発／エッセー

 次の英文を読んで、内容を理解しましょう。　　[学習目標時間30分]

●まず、以下の英文を4分半を目標に読んでみましょう。次ページの「単語のヘルプ」も、必要に応じて参考にしてください。

One of the most common causes of failure is the habit of quitting when one is overtaken by temporary defeat. Every person is guilty of this mistake at one time or another.

An uncle of R.U. Darby was caught by the "gold fever" in the gold-rush days, and went west to DIG AND GROW RICH. He had never heard that more gold has been mined from the brains of men than has ever been taken from the earth. He staked a claim and went to work with pick and shovel. The going was hard, but his lust for gold was definite.

After weeks of labor, he was rewarded by the discovery of the shining ore. He needed machinery to bring the ore to the surface. Quietly, he covered up the mine, retraced his footsteps to his home in Williamsburg, Maryland, told his relatives and a few neighbors of the "strike." They got together money for the needed machinery, had it shipped. The uncle and Darby went back to work the mine.

The first car of ore was mined, and shipped to a smelter. The returns proved they had one of the richest mines in Colorado! A few more cars of that ore would clear the debts. Then would come the big killing in profits.

Down went the drills! Up went the hopes of Darby and Uncle! Then something happened! The vein of gold ore disappeared! They had come to the end of the rainbow, and the pot of gold was no longer there! They drilled on, desperately trying to pick up the vein again — all to no avail.

Finally, they decided to QUIT.

They sold the machinery to a junk man for a few hundred dollars, and took the train back home. Some "junk" men are dumb, but not this one! He called in a mining engineer to look at the mine and do a little calculating. The engineer advised that the project had failed because the owners were not familiar with "fault lines." His calculations showed that the vein would be found JUST THREE FEET FROM WHERE THE DARBYS HAD STOPPED DRILLING! That is exactly where it was found!

The junk man took millions of dollars in ore from the mine, because he knew enough to seek expert counsel before giving up.

Three Feet from Gold from *Think and Grow Rich* by Napoleon Hill

---

Unit
18

単語のヘルプ

他にもわからないものがあったら辞書で調べて書き足しておきましょう。

☐ overtake 襲いかかる

☐ temporary 一時的な

☐ guilty of ～ ～に罪悪感を抱いた

☐ gold fever 金鉱熱

☐ dig 掘る

☐ mine 採掘する

☐ stake a claim 権利を主張する

☐ pick つるはし

☐ going 状況

- ☐ lust 欲望
- ☐ definite 疑いの余地がない
- ☐ reward 報いる
- ☐ ore 鉱石
- ☐ cover up 覆い隠す
- ☐ retrace （道を）引き返す
- ☐ footstep 足跡
- ☐ strike 大発見
- ☐ ship 出荷する
- ☐ smelter 製錬所
- ☐ returns 収益
- ☐ clear （借金を）返済する
- ☐ killing 大儲け、大当たり
- ☐ profit 利益
- ☐ vein 鉱脈
- ☐ pot of gold 夢のような幸運
- ☐ desperately 必死に
- ☐ pick up 獲得する
- ☐ to no avail 無駄に
- ☐ junk man 廃品回収業者
- ☐ dumb まぬけ
- ☐ call in 迎え入れる
- ☐ fault line 断層線
- ☐ millions of ～ 何百万もの～
- ☐ counsel 助言

TASK

2 読んだ英文の内容を他の人に話せるように英語でまとめ、また、ここから学べる教訓も付け、150語程度で以下に書きましょう（解答例は p. 232）。

_____

_____

_____

_____

_____

_____

_____

_____

_____

_____

_____

_____

_____

_____

Unit
18

I've just read an interesting story. In the days of gold rush, everybody was caught by the "gold fever" and the story was about one of those men. While working at a mining site, the man and his uncle discovered something shining in the earth. It was an ore. They borrowed money from relatives and neighbors to buy machinery needed to dig it from the ground. They found gold! It was a good start. But after that, however hard they drilled, they could not find any more gold. So they sold the machinery to a junk collector and left the site. But the collector was wise enough to take advice from an expert, and he actually started drilling himself. He found more gold only three feet away from the point where the man and his uncle had stopped.

An important lesson I learned from the story was: Get some advice from experts before giving up.

日本語訳

おもしろい話を読みました。ゴールドラッシュのころ、誰もが「金鉱熱」に浮かされていましたが、そんな一人の男の話です。発掘現場で作業をしていたその男性とおじは、地中に光るものを見つけました。鉱石でした。二人は親戚や近所の人たちから借金をして、それを掘り出すために必要な機械類を買いました。そして、金を見つけました！　好調な滑り出しでした。しかし、そのあとはどれだけ懸命に掘っても、金が出ることはもうありません。そこで、二人は機械類を廃品回収者に売り、現場をあとにしました。しかし、その回収者は賢いことに専門家から助言を受け、自ら掘削を始めました。最終的に男とそのおじが（掘るのを）やめた場所からほんの3フィート先のところに、より一層多くの金を見つけたのです。

この話から私が得た大切な教訓は、「あきらめる前に専門家に助言を求めよ」というものです。

音声でも聞いてみましょう。

 36

3 読み方のコツ

アメリカの自己啓発書の祖、ナポレオン・ヒル (1883〜1970) による作品の要約です。

● 使役の have

had it shipped（第3段落下から2〜1行目）

の have は「使役の have」。have ＋ A (目的語) ＋ B (過去分詞) の形で、「A を B の状態にしてもらう」の意味を表します。同じ語順で、

I had my purse stolen.（財布を盗まれた）

のように「A を B の状態にされる」を表す「被害の have」もあり、どちらの用法であるかは文脈から判断します。

● 倒置

強調したり、文章の調子を整えたりするときに使われる方法が倒置です。

Then would come the big killing in profits.（第4段落下から2〜1行目）

は、直前の A few more cars of that ore would clear the debts.（借金清算となる）に対して、「そのあとやってくるのは大儲けだ」と次に起きることを強調するために倒置を使っています。また、

Down went the drills! Up went the hopes of Darby and Uncle!（第 5 段落1行目）

は、down と up を対比させた躍動感あふれる2文にするために主語と動詞部分の位置を逆にしています。どちらも

Then the big killing in profits would come.

The drills went down! The hopes of Darby and Uncle went up!

と普通の語順にしてしまうと、この文章が持つべきリズムが失われてしまいます。

Unit
18

● 他動詞の work

How long have you been working here? や This printer doesn't work. のように work を自動詞で使うことがほとんどの方にとって、

The uncle and Darby went back to work the mine.（第3段落最終行）

の work はやや目新しい用法かもしれません。work at the mine ではない点に注意。work the mine で「鉱山を発掘する」を表します。

このほか、work farmland（農地を耕す）、work a computer（コンピューターを操作する）、work a horse（馬を働かせる）、work miracles（奇跡を起こす）など、目的語の機能を引き出すといったイメージで使われる他動詞 work も覚えておきましょう。

会話の幅を広げましょう!

第5段落2〜4行目のThey had come to the end of the rainbow, and the pot of gold was no longer there!は、There is a golden pot the end of the rainbow. (虹のふもとには黄金の壺がある) という言い伝えを応用したものです。「金鉱を掘っていた二人はすでに虹のふもと (the end of the rainbow) にまで来ていたが、もうそこには (有名な言い伝えではあるとされている) 黄金の壺はなかった」と言っています。うまく意味がつながらないと感じたときには、こうした伝説やことわざ、格言が基になっているのかもしれません。一度、調べてみるといいでしょう。

 1870年代頃、コロラド州はゴールド＆シルバー・ラッシュに湧きました。

よりよく英文を理解するために音声を使って学びます。ポーズの箇所で、意味を考えながら、繰り返し口に出してみましょう。

 37

One of the most common causes of failure is / the habit of quitting when one is overtaken by temporary defeat. // Every person is guilty of this mistake at one time or another. //

An uncle of R.U. Darby was caught by the "gold fever" in the gold-rush days, / and went west to DIG AND GROW RICH. // He had never heard that / more gold has been mined from the brains of men / than has ever been taken from the earth. // He staked a claim and went to work with pick and shovel. // The going was hard, but his lust for gold was definite. //

After weeks of labor, / he was rewarded by the discovery of the shining ore. // He needed machinery to bring the ore to the surface. // Quietly, he covered up the mine, / retraced his footsteps to his home in Williamsburg, Maryland, / told his relatives and a few neighbors of the "strike." // They got together money for the needed machinery, / had it shipped. // The uncle and Darby went back to work the mine. //

The first car of ore was mined, and shipped to a smelter. // The returns proved they had one of the richest mines in Colorado! // A few more cars of that ore would clear the debts. // Then would come the big killing in profits. //

Down went the drills! // Up went the hopes of Darby and Uncle! // Then something happened! // The vein of gold ore disappeared! // They had come to the end of the rainbow, / and the pot of gold was no longer there! // They drilled on, / desperately trying to pick up the vein again / —all to no avail. //

Finally, they decided to QUIT. //

Unit 18

They sold the machinery to a junk man for a few hundred dollars, / and took the train back home. // Some "junk" men are dumb, / but not this one! // He called in a mining engineer to look at the mine and do a little calculating. // The engineer advised that / the project had failed, / because the owners were not familiar with "fault lines." // His calculations showed that / the vein would be found / JUST THREE FEET FROM WHERE THE DARBYS HAD STOPPED DRILLING! // That is exactly where it was found! //

The junk man took millions of dollars in ore from the mine, / because he knew enough to seek expert counsel / before giving up. //

日本語訳

失敗の最も一般的な原因の一つは、一時的な敗北感に襲われると物事をやめてしまうという習慣である。だれもが一度や二度はこうした間違いを犯している。

R・U・ダービーの叔父は、ゴールドラッシュの時代に「金鉱熱」にとらわれ、採掘して金持ちになるために西へと向かった。土の中から採取されるより、人間の思考からのほうがより多くの金が採掘されたという話はそれまでに聞いたことがなかった。彼はそれは自分のものであると主張し、つるはしとシャベルを使った作業へと向かった。進行状況は大変だったが、彼の金への欲望は揺るぎないものだった。

数週間の労働の後、彼は輝く鉱石の発見によって報われた。彼にはその鉱石を地表まで出してくるための機械が必要だった。人目につかぬよう、彼は鉱床を隠し、来た道をたどってメリーランド州ウィリアムズバーグの自宅へ戻り、親戚や近所の人たちにその「大発見」のことを話した。彼らは必要な機械を買うためのお金を集めて、その機械を出荷した。叔父とダービーは発掘の仕事に戻った。

最初の運搬車両1台分の鉱石が採鉱され、精錬所に送られた。そこから得られた利益は、彼らがコロラドで最も豊かな鉱山の1つを持っていることを証明するものだった！ その鉱石をあと運搬車両2、3台分あれば借金は帳消しになるだろう。そして、大きな儲けが手に入るだろう。

掘削機を地中に下ろす！ ダービーと叔父さんの希望が高まる！ すると、何かが起こった！ 金鉱の鉱脈が消えたのだ！ 彼らは（黄金入りの壺があると言われる）虹のふもとまで来ていたのに、金の壺はもうそこにはなかったのだった！ 彼らは掘り続けて、懸命に鉱脈を捉えようとしたが、まったくの無駄だった。

ついに彼らはやめることにした。

数百ドルで廃品回収業者に機械を売って、列車に乗って帰路に着いた。廃品回収業者の中には愚かな者もいるが、この男は違った！　彼は鉱山技師を呼び、鉱山を見て計算をしてもらったのだった。技術者は、プロジェクトが失敗したのは所有者が「断層線」のことをよく知らなかったからだと助言した。彼の計算によると、その鉱脈はダービーが発掘をやめたところからわずか3フィートのところにあるとのこと！　そして、鉱脈はまさにそこから発見されたのだった！

その廃品回収業者は鉱山から何百万ドル分もの鉱石を採取したが、それは彼があきらめる前に専門家の助言を求めるという見識が十分にあったからなのである。

ナポレオン・ヒル著『思考は現実化する』「金鉱まで残り3フィート」より

Unit
18

英文の内容について以下の問いに答えましょう。

Q1 Who did the drilling with R.U. Darby?
    (A) The neighbors
    (B) A junk man
    (C) A mining engineer
    (D) His uncle

Q2 What did the junk man find after digging three more feet?
    (A) A fault line
    (B) A drill
    (C) A mine
    (D) A vein

解答と解説

Q1 解答（D）
R・U・ダービーと一緒に発掘を行なったのは誰ですか?
(A) 近所の人たち
(B) 廃品回収業者
(C) 鉱山技師
(D) おじ

解説 第2段落に、彼のおじさんがゴールドラッシュに魅了されて発掘に向かったとあり、第3段落最後の The uncle and Darby went back to work the mine. から、実際に発掘に行っていたのは、R・U・ダービー本人とそのおじさんであることがわかります。したがって、正解は (D) です。

Q2 解答（D）
廃品回収業者がさらに3フィート掘った後に見つけたものは何ですか?
(A) 断層線
(B) 掘削機
(C) 鉱山
(D) 鉱脈

解説 第7段落に廃品回収業者の行動が書かれています。下から3行目以降の ... the vein would be found JUST THREE FEET FROM WHERE THE DARBYS HAD STOPPED DRILLING! That is exactly where it was found! から、3フィート掘り進んだところには鉱脈があったとわかります。したがって、正解は (D) です。鉱山（mine）は掘削作業を行った場所全体を指しているので、(C) は答えとして適切ではありません。

Unit
18

英語の勉強も、目標を決めて
あきらめないことが大切！

38

| 難易度 ●●●●● 5 | | 約470語（長い） | | 小説紹介／書評 |

1 次の英文を読んで、内容を把握しましょう。　　　［ **学習目標時間40分** ］

● まず、以下の英文を5分を目標に読んでみましょう。次ページの「単語のヘルプ」
も、必要に応じて参考にしてください。

Book Review
The German Grandfather

Partway through Noah Barrington's debut novel, you might begin to sense that something is missing. His novel, *The German Grandfather*, is the story of Alan Veidt, the American-born son of German immigrants. Alan has known all his life that his grandparents chose to abandon postwar Germany with his young father. But now in his 40s, with both of his grandparents dead and his father's childhood stories vague and sometimes contradictory, Alan has decided to travel to his family's hometown of Kassel, Germany, to track down more information about his grandparents. Naturally, things do not go as expected. As he struggles with the language, German bureaucracy and discouraging family members, he also uncovers more questions and doubts surrounding what kind of man his grandfather really was.

This might sound familiar. There is, after all, no shortage of books and films about the gray moral areas that people sometimes occupied to simply survive the war. But what makes Barrington's book stand out in this crowded genre is that it never actually resorts to wartime flashbacks. *The German Grandfather* is a novel about Alan's journey into an uncertain relationship with his own history, and it is, from beginning to end, almost stubbornly contemporary.

Each piece of information Alan discovers is held at arm's length from the reader, making the meaning of these discoveries as secondhand and vague for us as it is for the book's main character. Barrington's writing is dense at times, and there is a touch of modernism to it, which may not be to everyone's taste. However, as Alan's increasingly paranoid thoughts take on lives of their own, it can be difficult to tell reality from his troubled imagination. Alan is a man watching his own history shift before his very eyes, and Barrington's uncertain, ever-shifting prose carries the reader along a similar path, adjusting and readjusting not only our understanding of past events but of Alan's own fragile sense of self. It is as though he is experiencing a kind of researcher's butterfly effect, in which each crumbling notebook and military record he consults alters his understanding of the present.

In the end, *The German Grandfather* is more interested in history's effects on the individual and the family than it is in the history itself. So if you're looking for a historical novel about World War II, this won't be for you. But Barrington turns a curious eye on the way that history is reflected in the present day and the shattering effect it can have on people and families that are unprepared to face difficult revelations. And that, ultimately, is what makes this novel very much worth the journey.

単語のヘルプ

他にもわからないものがあったら辞書で調べて書き足しておきましょう。
- [ ] partway through～ ～の途中で
- [ ] debut デビュー
- [ ] immigrant 移民
- [ ] abandon 捨てる
- [ ] contradictory 矛盾する
- [ ] track down 見つけ出す
- [ ] struggle with～ ～に苦労する
- [ ] bureaucracy 官僚主義
- [ ] discouraging 気持ちを落胆させるような

Unit
19

- ☐ uncover 明らかにする
- ☐ surrounding 〜 〜をめぐる
- ☐ shortage 不足
- ☐ gray area どちらともとれる領域、グレーゾーン
- ☐ occupy 占める
- ☐ stand out 目立つ
- ☐ genre ジャンル
- ☐ resort to 〜 〜という手段に訴える
- ☐ stubbornly 頑として
- ☐ contemporary 現代的な
- ☐ hold ... at arm's length …をやや距離のあるところに置く
- ☐ secondhand 間接の、また聞きの
- ☐ dense （文章などが）難解な
- ☐ at times 時々
- ☐ modernism 現代的思考
- ☐ taste 好み、嗜好
- ☐ paranoid 偏執性の
- ☐ take on a life of one's own 独り歩きする
- ☐ troubled 問題を抱えた
- ☐ ever-shifting 絶え間なく変化する
- ☐ prose 散文
- ☐ fragile もろい、脆弱な
- ☐ butterfly effect バタフライ効果
- ☐ crumbling 崩れかかっている
- ☐ military record 軍記
- ☐ consult 調べる
- ☐ alter 変える
- ☐ turn a curious eye on 〜 〜に好奇心に満ちた目を向ける
- ☐ shattering （希望などを）打ち砕くような
- ☐ unprepared 準備ができていない
- ☐ revelation 暴露された事実
- ☐ ultimately 結局、究極的に

TASK

2 書評を読んだ後に、この本を購入するかどうかを考えます。あなた自身の判断を理由とともに80語前後の英語で書いてみましょう。p. 245の「読み方のコツ」を参考にしても結構です（解答例はp. 244）。

☐ I'll (definitely) buy this book. _____

_____
_____
_____
_____
_____
_____
_____

☐ I don't think I'll buy this book. _____

_____
_____
_____
_____
_____
_____
_____

Unit
19

購入する

I'll definitely buy this book. His grandfather must have gone through a lot and I would like to know how people's minds worked in such a situation. I think it's good and even necessary to prepare for difficult times, if not for a wartime, and the book can give us some tips or food for thought. I read books of many genres, from philosophy and social science to literature and history. I think this book will cover all. That's another reason I would find this book worth reading.（私は絶対にこの本を買います。彼のおじいさんはいろいろなことを経験してきたはずですし、そうした状況において人の心がどのように動くのかを知りたいと思っています。戦時とは言わないまでも、大変な時代に備えることはいいことですし、必要であるとさえ思いますから、この本はいくらかのヒントや考える糧を与えてくれる可能性があります。私は、哲学から社会科学、文学、歴史にいたるまで、多くのジャンルの本を読みます。この1冊はすべてを網羅しそうです。それが、この本に読む価値があると考えるもうひとつの理由です）

購入しない

I don't think I'll buy this book. First, I'm not interested in wartime history. I know the way the book looks at history is quite different from conventional books, but the story sounds quite complicated, so it doesn't appeal to me. Next, if the language is difficult, as suggested in the review, it will take more time and effort to read. I read books for pleasure, not for torture. But I might take a quick look at it if someone lends it to me.（私はこの本は買いません。まず、戦時中の歴史に興味がないのです。歴史に対するこの本の視点が従来の本とはかなり異なることはわかっていますが、話がかなり複雑になりそうなので、興味を引かれません。それから、書評に示されているように言葉が難しければ、読むのに時間と努力が余計にかかります。私は楽しみのために読書をするのであって、苦しみのためにするのではありません。ただ、だれかが貸してくれるのであれば、さっと目を通すかもしれません）

3 読み方のコツ

● 離れた文言のつながりに気づく

すべてが同じ文、同じ段落の中で完結するわけではありません。こうした文章では、やや離れた文言をつなげることで全体をうまくまとめるという方法が使われます。第1段落1～2行目で、

you might begin to sense that something is missing（何かが欠けていると感じ始めるかもしれない）

とありますが、段落の残りにはあらすじが書かれているだけで、このmissingの具体的な内容は明らかにされていません。そこで読み進めていくと、

it never actually resorts to wartime flashbacks（第2段落4～5行目）

と、従来の歴史書にあるものがこの本にはないことが、また、

In the end, *The German Grandfather* is more interested in history's effects on the individual and the family than it is in the history itself. So if you're looking for a historical novel about World War II, this won't be for you.（第4段落1～4行目）

と、ここでもいわゆる普通の歴史書に期待する内容がないと書かれいて、これがmissingの指すことだと理解できます。先を読んでみて初めてわかることもあるという例です。

● 想像力を駆使して読む

話の流れを想像しながら読む部分では、自分なりに具体例を思い描いてみるといいでしょう。たとえば、

the gray moral areas that people sometimes occupied to simply survive the war（第2段落2～3行目）

は、平時では行なわない道徳上ギリギリのこと（たとえば、自宅の水道が戦火により止まってしまい、赤ん坊のミルクが作れないときに、他人の留守宅の井戸水を少しだけ無断で拝借するなど）をgray moral areasで表しています。

resorts to wartime flashbacks（第2段落4～5行目）

については、映画で戦時中の記録映像が差し込まれるシーンを思い浮かべるといいでしょう。また、

crumbling notebook and military record（第3段落下から2～1行目）

では、いきなりcrumbling（崩れかけた）という単語が出てきますが、主人公が時を経てボロボロになった状態のノートなどの資料をあたっている姿を思い浮かべられるでしょう。

Unit
19

domino effect（ドミノ効果）、echo effect（反響効果）、ripple effect（波及効果）、snowball effect（雪だるま効果）、trickle-down effect（トリクルダウン効果）などは、英語または日本語訳を見れば、「聞いたことがある」「何となく意味がかわる」といったものばかりですが、第3段落の下から2行目の butterfly effect（バタフライ効果）は名称からは、その意味するところがピンとこない表現です。これは、「ある場所で蝶が羽ばたくといずれ他の場所に嵐が起きる」という比喩を用いた、わずかな違いがのちにまったく別のところで大きな影響を及ぼすとする理論です。「風が吹けば桶屋が儲かる」とは異なり、途中で起きる事象の因果関係ははっきりとは示されません。

よりよく英文を理解するために音声を使って学びます。ポーズの箇所で、意味を考えながら、繰り返し口に出してみましょう。

🎧 38

The German Grandfather //

Partway through Noah Barrington's debut novel, / you might begin to sense that something is missing. // His novel, *The German Grandfather*, is the story of Alan Veidt, / the American-born son of German immigrants. // Alan has known all his life that / his grandparents chose to abandon postwar Germany with his young father. // But now in his 40s, / with both of his grandparents dead / and his father's childhood stories vague and sometimes contradictory, / Alan has decided to travel to his family's hometown of Kassel, Germany, / to track down more information about his grandparents. // Naturally, things do not go as expected. // As he struggles with the language, / German bureaucracy and discouraging family members, / he also uncovers more questions and doubts / surrounding what kind of man his grandfather really was. //

This might sound familiar. // There is, after all, no shortage of books and films about the gray moral areas / that people sometimes occupied to simply survive the war. // But what makes Barrington's book stand out in this crowded genre is that / it never actually resorts to wartime flashbacks. // *The German Grandfather* is a novel about Alan's journey / into an uncertain relationship with his own history, / and it is, from beginning to end, / almost stubbornly contemporary. //

Unit
19

Each piece of information Alan discovers is held at arm's length from the reader, / making the meaning of these discoveries / as secondhand and vague for us / as it is for the book's main character. // Barrington's writing is dense at times, / and there is a touch of modernism to it, / which may not be to everyone's taste. / However, / as Alan's increasingly paranoid thoughts take on lives of their own, / it can be difficult to tell reality from his troubled imagination. // Alan is a man watching his own history shift before his very eyes, / and Barrington's uncertain, ever-shifting prose carries the reader along a similar path, / adjusting and readjusting not only our understanding of past events / but of Alan's own fragile sense of self. // It is as though he is experiencing a kind of researcher's butterfly effect, / in which each crumbling notebook and military record he consults / alters his understanding of the present. //

In the end, / *The German Grandfather* is more interested in history's effects on the individual and the family / than it is in the history itself. // So if you're looking for a historical novel about World War II, / this won't be for you. // But Barrington turns a curious eye / on the way that history is reflected in the present day / and the shattering effect it can have on people and families / that are unprepared to face difficult revelations. // And that, ultimately, is what makes this novel / very much worth the journey. //

日本語訳

書評
『ドイツ人の祖父』

　ノア・バリントンのデビュー小説を読んでいると、その途中で何かが欠けていると感じ始めるかもしれない。彼の小説『ドイツ人の祖父』は、ドイツ移民の息子でアメリカ生まれのアラン・ヴェイトの物語である。アランは生まれてからずっと、祖父母が若かりしころの彼の父親と一緒に戦後のドイツを去る選択をしたことを知っていた。しかし、40歳代になった今、祖父母がともに亡くなり、父の子ども時代の物語があいまいで時には矛盾していたこともあって、アランは祖父母についてもっと知るために、家族の故郷であるドイツのカッセルに行くことにした。当然、物事は期待通りにはいかない。言語、ドイツの官僚主義、思いとどまらせようとする家族と格闘するうちに、彼はまた、祖父が本当はどんな人間だったのかについての疑問や疑念も明らかにしていく。

　これは聞き覚えがある話かもしれない。なにせ、人々が単に戦争を生き延びるために時に身を置いた道徳上のグレーゾーンに関する本や映画には事欠かない。しかし、数多くの作品を有するこのジャンルでバリントンの本が際立っているのは、戦時中の回想場面に頼ることがまったくないという点だ。『ドイツ人の祖父』は、アランが自身の歴史との不確かな関係をさぐる旅についての小説であり、最初から最後まで、ほとんど頑なに現代を舞台としている。

　アランが発見する一つひとつの情報は、読者からやや距離を置いたところにあるため、こうした発見の意味は、本書の主人公にとっても、私たちにとっても間接的であいまいなものになっている。バリントンの作品は時に難解で、わずかにモダニズムを感じさせるが、そうした作風は万人受けす

るものではない。しかし、次第に偏執的となるアランの思考が独り歩きするつれて、問題の多い彼の想像力から現実を区別しづらくなる可能性がある。アランは自分自身の歴史がまさに目の前で変化するのを見ている男であり、バリントンの書く不確かで絶えず変化する散文が、過去の出来事についての私たちの理解だけでなく、アラン自身の壊れやすい自我をも調整そして再調整しながら、読者を同様の流れに乗せて運ぶ。それはまるで研究者のバタフライ効果を体験しているかのようで、そこではボロボロになったノートと軍の記録を調べるたびに、彼の現在に対する理解が変わる。

　結局、『ドイツ人の祖父』は歴史そのものよりも、歴史が個人や家族に与える影響に関心を寄せた作品である。なので、第二次世界大戦についての歴史小説を探している人に向けたものではない。しかしバリントンは、歴史がどのように現在に反映されているか、そして、困難な事実に直面する準備ができていない人々や家族に、歴史がもたらす破壊的な影響に好奇の目を向けている。そして、最終的には、そのことがこの小説を（読書体験という）旅に十二分に見合うだけの価値があるものにしている。

Unit
19

英文の内容について以下の問いに答えましょう。

Q1 What is unique about the book, compared with ones with similar themes?
(A) It is not filled with scenes from the past.
(B) It fails to discuss the gray moral areas.
(C) It is more about the German language and bureaucracy.
(D) It is related with World War II.

Q2 What does the author put a main focus on?
(A) What lessons people learn from history
(B) Who are responsbile for the past wars
(C) Where his grandparents lived during the war
(D) How individuals are affected by history

解答と解説

Q1 解答（A）
この本が、同様のテーマの他の本と違うところはどこですか?
(A) 回想場面ばかりではない。
(B) 道徳的にどっちつかずの領域について語ってはいない。
(C) どちらかと言えばドイツ語とドイツの官僚制度に関するものである。
(D) 第二次世界大戦に関係している。

解説 第 2 段落 3〜5 行目に、what makes Barrington's book stand out in this crowded genre is that it never actually resorts to wartime flashbacks と書かれています。設問の unique はこの stand out を言い換えたもの。flashbacks に頼らないとは、過去の回想場面を多用しないということなので、正解は (A) です。

Q2 解答（D）
作者は何に主眼を置いていますか?
(A) 人々が歴史からどんな教訓を得るのか
(B) 誰が過去の戦争の責任者なのか
(C) 彼の祖父母が戦時中どこに住んでいたか
(D) 個人がいかに歴史に影響を受けているか

解説 第 4 段落 1〜2 行目の In the end, *The German Grandfather* is more interested in history's effects on the individual and the family than it is in the history itself. から、歴史が個人とその家族にどう影響するかに興味を示していることがわかるので、正解は (D) です。

最後の Unit です。
頑張ろう！

39

難易度 ●●●● 4 | 約600語（長い） | 物語抜粋／小説

 次の英文を読んで、内容を把握しましょう。　　[学習目標時間 30分]

●まず、以下の英文を7分を目標に読んでみましょう。次ページの「単語のヘルプ」も、必要に応じて参考にしてください。

I couldn't see my old man anywhere. One horse knee-ed himself up and the jock had hold of the bridle and mounted and went slamming on after the place money. The other horse was up and away by himself, jerking his head and galloping with the bridle rein hanging and the jock staggered over to one side of the track against the fence. Then Gillford rolled over to one side off my old man and got up and started to run on three legs with his off hoof dangling and there was my old man lying there on the grass flat out with his face up and blood all over the side of his head. I ran down the stand and bumped into a jam of people and got to the rail and a cop grabbed me and held me and two big stretcher bearers were going out after my old man and around on the other side of the course I saw three horses, strung way out, coming out of the trees and taking the jump.

My old man was dead when they brought him in and while a doctor was listening to his heart with a thing plugged in his ears I heard a shot up the track that meant they'd killed Gillford. I lay down beside my old man when they carried the stretcher into the hospital room and hung onto the stretcher and cried and cried and he looked so white and gone and so awfully dead and I couldn't help feeling that if my old man was dead maybe they didn't need to have shot Gillford. His hoof might have got well. I don't know. I loved my old man so much.

Then a couple of guys came in and one of them patted me on the back and then went over and looked at my old man and then pulled a sheet off the cot and spread it over him; and the other was telephoning in French for them to send the ambulance to take him out to Maisons. And I couldn't stop crying, crying and choking, sort of, and George Gardner came in and sat down beside me on the floor and put his arm around me and says, "Come on Joe old boy. Get up and we'll go out and wait for the ambulance."

George and I went out to the gate and I was trying to stop bawling and George wiped off my face with his handkerchief and we were standing back a little ways while the crowd was going out of the gate and a couple of guys stopped near us while we were waiting for the crowd to get through the gate and one of them was counting a bunch of mutuel tickets and he said, "Well Butler got his all right."

The other guy said, "I don't give a good goddam if he did, the crook. He had it coming to him on the stuff he's pulled."

"I'll say he had," said the other guy and tore the bunch of tickets in two.

And George Gardner looked at me to see if I'd heard and I had all right and he said, "Don't you listen to what those bums said Joe. Your old man was one swell guy."

But I don't know. Seems like when they get started they don't leave a guy nothing.

My Old Man (excerpt) by E. Hemingway

単語のヘルプ

他にもわからないものがあったら辞書で調べて書き足しておきましょう。

☐ my old man （ここでは）父親

☐ knee oneself up　膝をついて立ち上がる　＊knee-ed（原文ママ）は、動詞 knee の過去形の kneed となるべきところ

☐ jock　騎手

☐ bridle　馬勒（馬具の一種）

☐ slam　打つ

- [ ] place money （競馬などでの）掛け金
- [ ] jerk グイッと上げる
- [ ] gallop 全速力で走る
- [ ] bridle rein 手綱
- [ ] stagger よろける
- [ ] track 馬場
- [ ] roll over 横転する
- [ ] hoof 蹄
- [ ] dangle ぶら下がる
- [ ] flat out ばったりと
- [ ] with one's face up 仰向けになって
- [ ] bump into ～ ～にぶつかる
- [ ] jam 雑踏
- [ ] rail 手すり
- [ ] stretcher bearer 担架を担ぐ人
- [ ] string 一列に並ぶ ＊strung は過去形・過去分詞形
- [ ] plug 栓で詰める
- [ ] gone 死んで
- [ ] can't help ...ing …せざるをえない
- [ ] pat ... on the back …の背中をポンと叩く
- [ ] cot 簡易ベッド
- [ ] choke 息がつまる
- [ ] bawl 叫ぶ
- [ ] wipe off 拭う
- [ ] bunch 束
- [ ] mutuel ticket 馬券
- [ ] don't give a good goddam まったく気にしない
- [ ] crook 詐欺師
- [ ] have it coming 自業自得である
- [ ] pull （悪事を）しでかす
- [ ] tear 引き裂く ＊tore は過去形
- [ ] bum 浮浪者、怠け者
- [ ] swell すばらしい

TASK

2 登場人物と、それが誰で、どんな行動をしたかを日本語で整理し、英語であらすじをまとめましょう（解答例は p. 256）。

登場人物	初出行	誰	言動
I (Joe)	l. 1	語り手	父親を事故で亡くした
	l.		
	l.		
	l.		
	l.		
	l.		
	l.		
	l.		
	l.		
	l.		
	l.		

あらすじ

_____

_____

_____

_____

_____

_____

_____

_____

_____

_____

Unit
20

登場人物	初出行	誰	言動
I (Joe)	l. 1	語り手	父親を事故で亡くした
my old man	l. 1	語り手の父親	事故で亡くなる
the jock	l. 2	競馬の騎手	落馬したが、再度乗馬し、走り去った
the jock	l. 4	競馬の騎手	落馬し、その馬だけが走り去った
Gillford	l. 5	馬	語り手の父親を圧死させ、のちに射殺された
a cop	l. 10	警官	父親の元に駆けつけようとする語り手を引き止めた
stretcher bearers	l. 11	担架を運ぶ人たち	語り手の父親を担架に乗せて運んだ
a doctor	l. 14	医者	語り手の父親を診察した
a couple of guys	l. 22	医療関係者	語り手の父親の搬送を担当した
George Gardner	l. 26	語り手とその父親の知り合い	語り手を慰めた
a couple of guys/ bums	l. 33	競馬に賭けていた客	語り手の父親をなじった

あらすじ

This is a story about a boy who witnessed an accident in a horse race that killed his beloved father. One of the horses fell down on the boy's father, who was knocked off and dead. The boy overheard a conversation between betters saying his father was a cheater so they didn't care about his death. George, his father's friend, consoled him by saying his father was a good person, but the boy thought that was not a point. (これは、愛する父親が命を落とした、競馬場での事故を目撃した男の子の話です。1頭の馬が転んで男の子の父親の上に覆い被さり、跳ね飛ばされた父親は死亡しました。男の子は、父親は詐欺師だったから死んでも気にしないという馬券を買った人たちの会話をふと耳にします。父親の友人のジョージは、お父さんはいい人だったと言って慰めてくれましたが、男の子はそこが大事なのではないと思ったのでした）

3 読み方のコツ

アメリカの小説家E. ヘミングウェイ（1899〜1961）が、フランスでの競馬の障害レースで一財産手にしようとする騎手の父と、その息子について著した短篇の一部です。機会を見つけて、ぜひ最初から通して読んでみてください。

● and でつながった長い文

語り口調で書かれているためか、andで情報が数珠つなぎになっていることに気づきます。たとえば、第1段落下から5行目以降に、

I ran down the stand and bumped into a jam of people and got to the rail and a cop grabbed me and held me and two big stretcher bearers were going out after my old man and around on the other side of the course I saw three horses, strung way out, coming out of the trees and taking the jump.

という長い文がありますが、これは、

I ran down the stand and bumped into a jam of people and got to the rail

and

a cop grabbed me and held me

and

two big stretcher bearers were going out after my old man

and

around on the other side of the course I saw three horses, strung way out, coming out of the trees and taking the jump.

と4文がandでつながれ、その中でさらに並列を表すandが使われているという構造です。

　これを一気に理解しようとすると頭が混乱するかもしれません。それぞれ上記のように意味のまとまりの単位で区切って考えてみるのも一つの手です。この文章には、ほかにもandが多用されている箇所があります。精読し、前後のつながりを確認しておくといいでしょう。

● 聞き慣れない表現の意味を推測する

全編を通して何度も出てくるmy old manのように、直訳だけでは本当の意味がわからない表現があります。読み進めていくと、my old manが事故で亡くなったことで、語り手は涙が止まらなかったり、その知り合いらしき人（ジョージ）に慰められたりするので、語り手はmy old manの身内であることが推測できます。さらに、第3段落下から2行目で、ジョージが語り手にold boyと呼びかけていることから、ジョーは少年でmy old manはその父親ではないかと考えられるとよりよいで

しょう。なお、この old は「年をとった」の意味ではなく、親愛の情を表す形容詞です。

　また、第4段落以降の2人組の話に出てくる got his all right、crook、had it coming to him on the stuff he's pulled などは、最後にそのうちのひとりが tore the bunch of tickets in two（チケットを二つに切り裂いた）ことから悪口ではないかと考えられます。その直後に、ジョージが悲しんでいるジョーに対し、Don't you listen to what those bums ...（あんな奴らの言うことは聞いてはいけない）と言っていることから、やはり悪口だったと確信できます。

 会話の幅を広げましょう!

この物語の最終文 Seems like when they get started they don't leave a guy nothing. では don't ... nothing と否定語が重なっています。これは、肯定を表す二重否定ではなく、否定のニュアンスを強める用法です。標準的文法に則れば、don't ... anything (at all) とすべきところですが、実際にはこうした形も使われています。今後学習を進めていく過程で、You don't know nothing about me.（あなたは私のことなんかひとつもわかっていない）や I won't tell nobody about this.（このことは決して誰にも言いません）といった文例に出会うこともあるでしょう。肯定なのか否定の強調なのかは、文脈に合うかどうかを基準に、柔軟に考えることが求められます。なお、この文では、if に even if の意味があるのと同様、when が「〜であるとしても」と譲歩を表している点にも注意しましょう。

4 よりよく英文を理解するために音声を使って学びます。ポーズの箇所で、意味を考えながら、繰り返し口に出してみましょう。

🎧 **39**

I couldn't see my old man anywhere. // One horse knee-ed himself up / and the jock had hold of the bridle and mounted and / went slamming on after the place money. // The other horse was up and away by himself, / jerking his head and galloping with the bridle rein hanging / and the jock staggered over to one side the track against the fence. // Then Gillford rolled over to one side off my old man / and got up and started to run on three legs / with his off hoof dangling / and there was my old man lying there on the grass flat out / with his face up and blood all over the side of his head. // I ran down the stand and bumped into a jam of people and got to the rail / and a cop grabbed me and held me / and two big stretcher bearers were going out after my old man / and around on the other side of the course / I saw three horses, strung way out, / coming out of the trees and taking the jump. //

My old man was dead when they brought him in / and while a doctor was listening to his heart with a thing plugged in his ears / I heard a shot up the track that meant they'd killed Gillford. // I lay down beside my old man when they carried the stretcher into the hospital room / and hung onto the stretcher and cried and cried / and he looked so white and gone and so awfully dead / and I couldn't help feeling that / if my old man was dead maybe they didn't need to have shot Gillford. // His hoof might have got well. // I don't know. // I loved my old man so much. //

Then a couple of guys came in / and one of them patted me on the back / and then went over and looked at my old man / and then pulled a sheet off the cot and spread it over him; / and the other was telephoning in French for them to send the ambulance / to take him out to Maisons. // And I couldn't stop crying, crying and choking, sort of, / and George Gardner came in and sat down beside me on the floor

Unit 20

/ and put his arm around me and says, / "Come on Joe old boy. // Get up and we'll go out and wait for the ambulance." //

George and I went out to the gate and I was trying to stop bawling / and George wiped off my face with his handkerchief / and we were standing back a little ways / while the crowd was going out of the gate / and a couple of guys stopped near us / while we were waiting for the crowd to get through the gate / and one of them was counting a bunch of mutuel tickets / and he said, "Well Butler got his all right." //

The other guy said, / "I don't give a good goddam if he did, the crook. // He had it coming to him on the stuff he's pulled." //

"I'll say he had," / said the other guy and tore the bunch of tickets in two. //

And George Gardner looked at me / to see if I'd heard and I had all right / and he said, / "Don't you listen to what those bums said Joe. // Your old man was one swell guy." //

But I don't know. // Seems like when they get started / they don't leave a guy nothing. //

日本語訳

父さんはどこにもいなかった。一頭の馬が膝をついて立ち上がると、騎手が馬勒をつかんで馬に乗り、むちを打ちながら賞金を目当てに走っていった。もう一頭の馬も、自力で立って頭をぐいと振り、手綱をぶら下げながら疾走していき、騎手は柵にぶつかって走路の片側へとよろめきながら歩いていった。するとギルフォードは、ゴロリと横に転がってぼくの父の上からどいた。立ち上がると一本の蹄（ひづめ）をだらりと垂らして三本足で走り始めたが、その芝生の上には父さんが仰向けにばったりと横たわっていて、頭の横一面に血を流していた。ぼくは観客席を駆け降りて、人垣にぶつかりながら、手すりのところまで着き、警官がぼくをつかんでおさえつけ、大きな2人の担架の運搬人がぼくの父さんのほうに向かってきて、コースの反対側の走路のあたりに、3頭の馬がずっと向こうで一列に並び、木立から出てきてジャンプしているのが見えた。

ぼくの父さんは運び込まれてきたときには死んでいて、医者が耳に何かものを詰めて父さんの心臓の音を聞いているときに、走路のほうで銃声が聞こえたが、それは彼らがギルフォードを射殺したことを意味していた。担架を病室に運んできたとき、ぼくは父さんのそばに身を横たえ、担架につかまって泣きに泣いたけど、父さんは顔色がすっかり白く、完全に死んでいた。もし父さんが死んでいるのなら、ギルフォードを撃つ必要はなかったのではないかと思わずにはいられなかった。彼の蹄は良くなったかもしれないのだし。それはわからない。ぼくは父さんをとても愛していた。

それから二人の男が入ってきて、そのうちの一人が私の背中を軽くたたいてから、向こうに行き、父さんを見て、簡易ベッドからシーツをはがし、父さんの上に広げてくれた。もう一人はフランス語で電

話をし、救急車をよこして父さんをメゾンまで搬送するよう言っていた。ぼくは涙が止まらず、いわば、泣いては喉を詰まらせていると、ジョージ・ガードナーが入ってきてぼくの横の床に座り、ぼくに腕を回して、「さあ、ジョー、いい子だ。立ち上がって、外で救急車を待とう」と言った。

ジョージとぼくは門のところに出て、泣き叫ぶのをこらえようとしていると、ジョージがハンカチでぼくの顔をぬぐい、ぼくたちが、群衆が門から出ていく中、少し後ろに立っていると、群衆が門を通り抜けるのを待っていたときに、二人の男たちがぼくたちの近くで立ち止まると、一人が馬券の束を数えて、「まあ、バトラーは自業自得だった」と言った。

もう一人は「おれはそうだったとしても、何とも思わないな、あの詐欺師の野郎。やつにとっては自分で蒔いた種だったんだ」と言った。

「そうだろうな」と相手の男は言い、馬券の束を二つに引き裂いた。

するとジョージ・ガードナーはぼくが聞いていたかを確かめようとこっちを見て、ぼくは聞いたと答えると、ジョージは「あんな能なしの言うことなんか聞くな、ジョー。お前の父さんは立派な男だった」と言った。

しかし、ぼくにはわからない。この世の中は、何かを始めたとしても、何もあとには残らないようだ。

E・ヘミングウェイ著『ぼくの父さん』（抜粋）

Unit
20

英文の内容について以下の問いに答えましょう。

Q1 How many horses were involved in the accident?
(A) One　　　(B) Two
(C) Three　　(D) Four

Q2 What did George Gardner mean when he said, "Your old man was one swell guy."?
(A) He was making a lot of money on business.
(B) He was cheating people and called a crook.
(C) He was a nice person despite the reputation.
(D) He was good at selling tickets to customers.

解答と解説

Q1　解答（C）
その事故には何頭の馬が巻き込まれましたか?
(A) 1頭　　　(B) 2頭
(C) 3頭　　　(D) 4頭

解説　第1段落1行目に One horse kneed-ed himself up と、3行目に The other horse was up とあり、ともに騎手が落馬したことから事故にあった馬だとわかります。また、5行目以降の Then Gillford rolled over ... started to run on three legs with his off hoof dangling からこの Gillford も馬であると判断できます。One horse の one と The other horse の the other から2頭ですべてだと考えがちですが、Gillford 以外に事故に巻き込まれた馬が「全部で2頭」いたという流れです。したがって、正解は (C) です。

Q2　解答（C）
ジョージ・ガードナーはどういう意味で Your old man was one swell guy. と言ったのですか?
(A) 仕事で多くの稼ぎがあった。
(B) 人を騙していて、ペテン師と呼ばれていた。
(C) 評判とは違っていい人だった。
(D) 客にチケットを売りさばくのがうまかった。

解説　第4〜6段落で、競馬場から出てきた2人組が Well Butler got his all right.（自業自得だ）、He had it coming to him on the stuff he's pulled.（自分の蒔いた種だ）などと捨て台詞を吐いていますが、それを聞いたジョージ・ガードナーが Don't you listen to what those bums said（あんなやつらの話は聞くな）に続けて設問のセリフを言っていることから、(C) が正解だとわかります。

Good job!

霜村和久

横浜国立大学、文京学院大学、明海大学非常勤講師。大手英会話学校、サイマル・インターナショナルプログラム開発室室長、ジャパンタイムズ書籍編集担当などを経て、独立。書籍執筆・翻訳、英語研修教材作成・指導などで、幅広く活躍。著書に、『iBT対応 TOEFL®テスト完全攻略 リーディング』（アルク）、『TOEIC® TEST やさしい文法レッスン』（アスク出版）、『Primary Grammar Lesson for the TOEIC® TEST』（センゲージラーニング）、『英語で論語』（祥伝社）、『ヤワらか英語アタマをつくる英作文教室』『よりぬき英語で読む日本昔ばなし』（以上、ジャパンタイムズ出版）などがある。

4-in-ONE シリーズ

『4-in-ONE advanced 上級』

発行日：2021年3月19日（初版）

著者：霜村和久
編集：株式会社アルク 書籍編集チーム
英文執筆：Braven Smillie ／Owen Schaefer
英文校正：Peter Branscombe ／Margaret Stalker
アートディレクション・本文デザイン：伊東岳美
イラスト：矢戸優一
ナレーション：Rachel Walzer ／Ryan Drees ／Josh Keller
音声録音・編集：株式会社メディアスタイリスト
DTP：朝日メディアインターナショナル株式会社
印刷・製本：日経印刷株式会社

発行者：天野智之
発行所：株式会社アルク
〒102-0073 東京都千代田区九段北4-2-6 市ヶ谷ビル
Website: https://www.alc.co.jp/